THE HOMECOMING THEME IN MODERN DRAMA

The Return of the Prodigal

"Guilt to be on Your Side"*

THE HOMECOMING THEME IN MODERN DRAMA

The Return of the Prodigal

"Guilt to be on Your Side"*

Leah Hadomi

The Edwin Mellen Press
Lewiston/Queenston/Lampeter

Library of Congress Cataloging-in-Publication Data

Hadomi, Leah.
    The homecoming theme in modern drama : the return of the prodigal
son : guilt to be on your side / Leah Hadomi.
        p.   cm.
    Includes bibliographical references (p.   ) and index.
    ISBN 0-7734-9578-9
    1. Drama--20th century--History and criticism. 2. Prodigal son
(Parable) in literature. I. Title. II. Title: Home coming theme
in modern drama.
PN1861.H27 1992
809.2'9355--dc20

                                                                    92-21862
                                                                        CIP

*"Guilt to be on Your Side" is a letter from Kafka to his father.

A CIP catalog record for this book
is available from the British Library.

All rights reserved. For information contact

The Edwin Mellen Press   The Edwin Mellen Press
        Box 450   Box 67
Lewiston, New York   Queenston, Ontario
    USA 14092   CANADA L0S 1L0

The Edwin Mellen Press, Ltd.
Lampeter, Dyfed, Wales
UNITED KINGDOM SA48 7DY

Printed in the United States of America

CONTENTS

I. INTRODUCTION

THE PRODIGAL RETURN AS AN ARCHI-PATTERN

The story of the prodigal son is structured as a variation on a widespread discourse about archetypal patterns of experience. This "situation humana" gave rise to works which centered on father/son and sibling relations; these expanded from the individual sphere to the social, including elements of generational revolt against the lifestyle of the forefathers.[1] The prodigal son's story of leaving home and return clusters elements of generational antagonism based on the concurrence of fragmentation and wholeness, the provisional and the eternal, and life and death as premises in its strategy.

The story of the prodigal son is archetypal, perceptible even through the various literary transfigurations which it has undergone with regard to setting, plot sequences, character types and other compositional elements. Therefore the story as a whole will be termed the "archi-pattern". This term leans on Jung, but also takes into consideration the social and historical variations in the prodigal son story and considers it as an hermeneutic code. The most popular prefiguration of the story is perhaps the one to be found in Luke 15: 11-32. This version is termed here "Ur-scene". In the following discussion the term "archi-pattern" will be used in reference to the universal, essential and typical characteristic of the prototype, and "Ur-scene" when the literary version of Luke should be considered. Because of its archetypal nature and its religious presentation, this story became a source of inspiration in literature, theatre and iconographic art alike. Secular postfigurations of the parable were very popular on the Continent in the 16th and 17th centuries, and are interwoven into artistic presentations up to the 20th.

The postfiguration of the prodigal son in literature tends to appear within a wider family context. Some authors present a text dominated or influenced by theology; others stress the social dimension, in which the vital harmony of the organic family structure is opposed to the universal society of *bellum omnium contra omnes*.[2] Psychological strata of parent-child relationships, as well as those between siblings, may be emphasised, or the existential domain may lead the configuration. However, all these approaches, which may appear in different combinations, deal with the archi-pattern of the son's return to his family. They are influenced by a historical-cultural code, in whose terms the archi-pattern is translated into a literary context.

The modern version of the archi-pattern is built on a model of self-referentiality. The innovation of the modern versions gains meaning only in reference to earlier ones, and the socio-cultural influences only gain meaning if they are reformulated into a literary entity. The postfiguration of the prodigal son archi-pattern in literature creates different degrees of awareness of the mythical layer within each work. Postfiguration of the archi-pattern can constitute the main or side cluster in the latter dramatic composition, or elements can be drawn from it and interwoven in the work. As J. J. White puts it: "Prefiguration arouses expectations in the reader which may or may not be fulfilled, and in any case will probably be satisfied in unexpected ways".[3] The archi-pattern, therefore, is constantly manipulated into further literary works.[4]

Any discussion of the historically bound dramatic presentation of the archi-pattern has also to take into consideration the dramatic and theatrical conventions which influenced this presentation. In Pavis' terms: "This quest for an aesthetic and social common ground, far from contradictions or conflict, certainly implies (as we shall see) a close link with heritage and tradition, because the motivating force of theatre — of the actor, designer, director — is not only cultural heritage (great authors, great classical texts, fundamental myths of social and symbolic life) but also the heritage of vocal, gestural and intonative practice".[5] Similar variations may also be traced in the dynamics of the theatrical presentation of the prodigal son archi-pattern. This structural concept of the pattern being reshaped in relation to the socio-cultural process creates a dynamic rhythm, in which the "signifier absorbs the new signified every time and gives rise to a new signifier, from which new signification emerges".[6]

This book serves a double function: a discussion of selected modern plays integrating the prodigal son archi-pattern, and an attempt to analyse analogies and differences between versions of the archi-pattern in these plays, as influenced by changes in literary, dramatic and socio-cultural codes. H. G. Gadamer proposes that we can understand a text only if we have understood the question to which the text is an answer, and that this question cannot be reconstructed in its original horizon, for this historical horizon is engulfed by our present one.[7] To make a detailed analysis of specific texts as well as the system of variants in a different historical horizon, it is appropriate to precede with a survey of the religious prefiguration of the archi-pattern and its literary development; the socio-cultural background to this secular postfiguration of modern dramatic versions, and an exposition of methodology.

THE BIBLICAL VERSION, OR THE UR-SCENE

As stated, the archi-pattern of father-son and sibling relationships, clustered around the return of the prodigal son, has its most comprehensive manifestation in the New Testament. The 'Ur-scene' in Luke 15: 11-32 is the intertextual core for further variations to be discussed:

> He also said "A man had two sons. The younger said to his father, "Father, let me have the share of the estate that would come to me". So the father divided the property between them. A few days later, the younger son got together everything he had and left for a distant country where he squandered his money on a life of debauchery.

> When he had spent it all, that country experienced a severe famine, and now he began to feel the pinch, so he hired himself out to one of the local inhabitants who put him on his farm to feed the pigs. And he would willingly have filled his belly with the husks the pigs were eating but no one offered him anything. Then he came to his senses and said, "How many of my father's paid servants have more food than they want, and here am I dying of hunger! I will leave this place and go to my father and say: Father, I have sinned against heaven and against you; I no longer deserve to be called your son; treat me as one of your paid servants". So he left the place and went back to his father.

> While he was still a long way off, his father saw him and was moved with pity. He ran to the boy, clasped him in his arms and kissed him tenderly. Then his son said, "Father, I have sinned heaven and against you. I no longer deserve to be called your son". But the father said to his servants, "Quick! Bring out the best robe and put it on him; put a ring on his finger and sandals on his feet. Bring the calf we have been fattening, and kill it; we are going to have a feast, a celebration, because this son of mine was dead and has come back to life; he was lost and is found". And they began to celebrate.

> Now the elder son was out in the fields, and on his way back, as he drew near the house, he could hear music and dancing. Calling one of the servants he asked what it was all about. "Your brother has come", replied the servant "and

your father has killed the calf we had fattened because he has got him back safe
and sound". He was angry then and refused to go in, and his father came out
to plead with him; but he answered his father, "Look, all these years I have
slaved for you and never once disobeyed your orders, yet you never offered me
so much as a kid for me to celebrate with my friends. But, for this son of yours,
when he comes back after swallowing up your property — he and his women
— you kill the calf we had been fattening".

The father said, "My son, you are with me always and all I have is yours. But
it was only right we should celebrate and rejoice, because your brother here
was dead and has come to life; he was lost and is found". (The Jerusalem Bible)

In Christian theology, as well as in various systems of text analysis,
there is an ongoing discussion as to whether this text should be treated as
a parable or as an analogy.[8] Does it, like a parable, emphasise religious
intentions pointing to the benevolence of God the Father, as opposed to
the sinners and to their joy when they are forgiven by God's love? Or is
it structured as an analogy for man's eternal strife, his fight against sin and
his attempt to return to innocence? Other interpretations of the Ur-scene
epitomise religious, literary, psychological, philosophical or historical
approaches. Here only representative examples will be mentioned.

Archbishop Trench explains two main Christian approaches: that of
the "Gentile and Jew" and that of the "penitent sinners and proud
sinners".[9] Julius Schniewind stresses the forgiveness and love of the father,
and finds this theological approach to be a continuation of the Old
Testament.[10] Joachim Jeremias, in his *Die Gleichnisse Jesus,* states that
the parable of the Prodigal Son should really be named the parable of the
Loving Father, as it stresses the love and benevolence of God. The
similarity of the endings of the two parts of the story, reaching a climax in
the second, stresses Jesus' justification of the sinner by the love of God.[11]
Karl Heinrich Rengstorf refers to the historical legalistic background to
"the lost" son, highlighting the thematic aspects of life and death, lost and
found. This background is to be understood as evolving from the Jewish
institution of *kesasah,* whose purpose was to expel the sinning son from the
community. The reconstitution of the son to his home and inheritance at
the end of the parable is symbolised on the basis of accepted rituals of
those times, involving garment, ring and shoes.[12] Alexander Belmain Bruce
stresses the textual interconnection between the three parables which

appear in the chapter: the lost sheep, the lost coin and the lost son. The meaning evolving from this interconnection is:

> Man, viewed as the object of the Saviour's solicitude, is lost as a straying sheep is lost, through thoughtlessness; as a piece of money is lost to use, when its owner cannot find it; as a prodigal is lost, who in waywardness and self-will departs from his father's house to a distant land.[13]

An existential approach can be seen in Geraint's analysis.[14] Existential motifs in the parable are freedom, responsibility, alienation, longing, grace, anguish and reconciliation. The identification with the characters of the parable exists because its artistic qualities speak with an eloquence that is not possible for propositional and doctrinal statements. There are various other analyses of the parable based on psychoanalytical, Jungian and literary approaches.[15] One of them is the contradiction between "the anomaly of the feted prodigal and the unfeted dutiful son",[16] which makes the story polyvalent and invites further variant theological and aesthetic interpretation. This multiplicity of readings in itself is evidence of the complexity and paradoxes of the text, which invite the reader to establish connections among elements.

THE DRAMATIC PRESENTATION

Aspects of Secularization

The literary development of the secular archi-pattern, based on the Ur-scene, developed in Europe in different versions, some of which have probably been lost. Some, like the verse story "Meier Helmbrecht" by Wernher der Gartneare, appeared in the 13th century, but the first dramatic presentations were in the Netherlands, France and Italy around 1500. Perhaps the best known of these is *Acolastus, de filio prodigo Comoedia* (by Gnapheus, the real name was Willem de Volder, 1529). Versions later appeared in other countries, including England.[17] The English versions developed from two dramatic traditions: the Christian Terence and the native morality plays. The first Continental play translated into English was *Acolastus* in 1540, and thereafter new English adaptations appeared. The popularity of the parable in England might have been furthered by the custom of reading it three times a year in church.

In the plays of the 16th and 17th century, a period which represents the peak of their popularity, the emphasis is on the central issue of God's grace as well as on the psychological aspect — the temptation and conversion of the younger son and the rivalry between the brothers. The dramatic presentations spread into other Western European countries, where both Catholics and Protestants supported them for religious and moral purposes. The character of the parable, with the father figure standing for

God and the lost son for Sin, made it popular for preaching.[18] Another cause of the wide reception of the plays was that their texts were used for Latin language instruction.[19]

The perceived meaning of the Ur-scene within the plays shifts with history. The main changes are that while in the Bible the main explicit motivation for the son's return is economic, in the Middle Ages his leaving home meant wickedness, religious or moral, which had to be punished, and the way home stood for repentance and forgiveness. The emphasis was on the atonement of the son or the conflict between the brothers more than on the benevolence of the father. The Reformist and bourgeois period emphasised the secular exemplar in the play while not abandoning the religious one. Tragic elements, which could not develop so long as the emphasis was parabolic, with a religious mission, could now be incorporated. The motivation for claiming the inheritance, the moral deterioration of the younger son, and the jealousy between the brothers all became more prominent. Further development of the dramatic form laid more stress on the homecoming, and plays began to omit the sections of the plot concerning the son's sins or his humiliation/defeat.[20] The growing emphasis on the homecoming was also caused by the de-emphasis of the moral aspect of guilt and repentance, which was replaced by other elements, most notably the theme of sibling envy. The two brothers began to gain individual characteristics: the elder one became a type of "Bürger", the younger, who left, an artist.

The archi-pattern's constant reappearance in literature, although often structured as a variation on the Ur-scene, demonstrates its historical and its cross-cultural vitality. The widespread belief in man's yearning to "come home" also appears in modern literature. In the 20th century, the motif is evident in prose writings by Gide, Kafka and Camus, where it has mainly been interpreted as the return of man to himself.[21] In another deviation from the standard ritual of the homecoming, the prodigal wants his family to accept him.[22] The ritual frames feelings of uncertainty and fear that the consequences of homecoming might be other than wished for. The expected ritualistic initiation into the family acquires an undercurrent of irony. The archi-pattern's modern manifestations, then, contain contextual and formal alternatives, but they all refer to the frame structure of the normative, conventional return home.

The relationship between the archi-pattern of the prodigal son and the dramatic texts discussed here is not solely based on the inclusion of material from the archi-pattern, or the reconstruction of Ur-scene in all its stages. The degree and character of the relationship between the archi-pattern and its postfiguration are set against a historical horizon. The aim of this analysis is to pinpoint the changes in content and dramatic form that the archi-pattern has undergone. The basic devices with which the archi-pattern of the prodigal son is expressed are the main characters, the pattern of the plot, and three major recurrent aspects of the theme horizon.

The symbolic figures in the archi-pattern are the father, the elder son who stays at home fulfilling his duties, and the returning, prodigal, younger son. In the Ur-scene the father is unambiguously forgiving and benevolent to the returning son, an iconisation of God's kindness and love. The two sons, however, are complicated figures even in this early version. The return of the prodigal is ambiguous; the cause for it is economic, but there is a confession of guilt — "Father, I have sinned", — which is seemingly elicited by his father's forgiving embrace. The elder son's jealousy of his brother might be straightforward envy of the latter's reception; but it could also be justifiable anger in the light of his loyalty to his father, as well as to the farm. This primal configuration, which already contained some ambiguity with regard to characters, underwent further changes as a result of secularisation of the archi-pattern and changes in the socio-cultural code. The hierarchic stratification of father and sons, and the emphasis on sin and forgiveness, vary considerably in the later versions. The brother/brother conflict becomes more prominent and is treated differently, and a female figure is introduced.

The other architectonic aspect of the Ur-scene is the plot sequence and the ways this sequence is co-ordinated. Young's division of the plot of the Ur-Scene into ten segments is helpful in discussing the more general variations which occur in the archi-pattern:

> The paradigm consists of ten clearly defined sequences of action: a request, the granting of the request, the journey into the far country, the riotous living, the loss of financial means and the consequent necessity to work, the accompanying humiliation and despair, the repentance and return, the generous reception, the celebration, and the elder brother's reaction with the ensuing riposte of the father.[23]

The first part of the plot's development, up to the point of return, is not particularly elaborated in the Ur-scene, a tendency which becomes more pronounced in later versions. The story of the son's riotous living and his humiliation and despair was de-emphasised, and its remnants appear as exposition.

The modern versions of the archi-pattern which will be discussed here alter some of these segments, omitting or reshuffling them, or adding new ones. We shall find that the first segments are omitted and the "repentance" and "return" segments coalesce into a problem of the "recognition" of the son by his family. The family situation which evolves as a result of the son's return is based on a "secret", which constitutes a new segment of plot.

The Theme Horizon

The thematic horizon of the archi-pattern contains three main elements: sin and forgiveness, lost and found, and death and life.[24] In the modern versions of the archi-pattern generally, these aspects become extended and transformed into guilt/innocence, inward/outward and death/life. These should not be understood as dichotomies; rather, each represents the twin poles of a cognitive and moral process.

Sin and forgiveness forms part of the conventional religious signifying system. The stable value system by which the behaviour of the son was judged only includes very narrow limits of ambiguity. The forgiveness of the father was total and unconditional. We might suggest that secularisation, and changes in modern life which include relativism of value hierarchies, necessitated the redefinition of the sin/forgiveness element. Its reappearance as guilt/innocence permits relativism and subjectivity.

The lost and found thematic element in the Ur-scene is emphasised by context — the parables of the lost and found sheep and the lost and found coin which introduce it:

> And he spake this parable unto them, saying, What man of you, having an hundred sheep, if he lose one of them, doth not leave the ninety and nine in the wilderness, and go after that which is lost, until he find it? And when he hath found it, he layeth it on his shoulders, rejoicing. And when he cometh home he calleth together his friends and neighbours, saying unto them, Rejoice with me; for I have found my sheep which was lost. I say unto you, that likewise joy shall be in heaven over one sinner that repenteth, more than over ninety and nine just persons, which need no repentance. Either what woman having ten pieces of silver, if she lose one piece, doth not light a candle, and sweep the house, and seek diligently till she find it? And when she hath found it, she calleth her friends and her neighbours together, saying, Rejoice with me; for I have found the piece which I had lost. Likewise, I say unto you, there is joy in the presence of the angels of God over one sinner that repenteth.

If we consider these parables, the re-emphasis that being lost is somehow to deviate from the norm is obvious. The Ur-scene develops this: the son is "lost" to sin and subsequently "found" — re-integrated into his family, his community values and his home. In the modern dramas, this element is transformed into an "inward/outward" aspect. The son is "lost" to sin and turns "outwards": his return "inward" to his home is motivated by memories of the past and the wish to be rehabilitated and re-integrated. A spatial as well as a temporal dimension is evident; the return home is a return to a space known because of past memories. These memories effectively take the place of the value system of the Ur-scene.

Death and life, in the Ur-scene, is also linked to sin, "because this son of mine was dead". The prodigal's return brings him back to life. In the modern versions, however, the inherent opposition in this thematic aspect becomes blurred; both "death" (outside the home) and "life" (within it) are marked by biological or material deterioration and/or instability. Both are ambiguous states. Therefore, the return of the son cannot directly imply "life", although, as we shall see, there may be hints of some kind of cyclic pattern in existence.

The assumption of this work is that the three thematic aspects are not durative, as such, in modern dramatic discourse on the prodigal son.

Meaning and textual structure are determined by period and author. The perspective of the prodigal pattern has changed, and the historicity of this change is the fusion of past conventions with present ones. It is self-evident therefore that an awareness of the prefiguration of characters, plot segments and thematic aspects of the prodigal son are essential for viewing the contextual and formal changes of the modern versions. As Gadamer puts it:

> Every age has to understand a transmitted text in its own way, for the text is part of the whole of the tradition in which the age takes an objective interest, and in which it seeks to understand itself.[25]

Methodological Remarks

The first part of this work will discuss six modern dramatic variations of the prodigal son archi-pattern, be this the main or the sub-theme of the drama. The choice has been limited to plays in English, based on the assumption that a coherent tradition enables better tracing of a literary theme. One exception is a play by Ibsen, who, as the father of modern drama, had a great influence on the contextual as well as the formal aspects of its development. The inclusion of *Ghosts* serves as a milestone to modern versions, particularly as Ibsen's influence on English and American dramatists was not only great, but acknowledged by many of them.[26] The dramas presented here are Ibsen's *Ghosts* (1881), O'Neill's *Long Day's Journey Into Night* (1941), Miller's *Death of a Salesman* (1949), Albee's *Who's Afraid of Virginia Woolf?* (1962), Pinter's *The Homecoming* (1965) and Shepard's *Buried Child* (1979). The plays are discussed in chronological order. "Former" and "later" are used as operative terms, though no systematic diachronic development is clearly evident. But a line of change that is noticeable in an overall diachronic view is the shift from realistic dramas to other modern dramatic configurations. For the convenience of this discussion, the six plays have been divided into two groups. The first, by Ibsen, O'Neill and Miller, have been termed "realistic plays" and the second, by Albee, Pinter and Shepard, have been termed "modernistic plays". There is a strong element of schematization in these groupings. In Miller's play, the staging of memories is an expressionistic device, breaking the conventions of naturalistic realism and bringing him closer to the second group. Albee's play still presents well-defined counters of *dramatis personae,* and a causal, explanatory plot. These two plays rightfully belong between the two groups, serving as a sort of transition. However, for the sake of a workable vocabulary, each play has been assigned to one of the two groups.

A methodological problem of sorts is the analysis of the individual texts inductively while still attempting to deduce the specific function the archi-pattern plays in each drama. This is further complicated when, in the Conclusion, all six dramas and their relationship to the archi-pattern will be considered simultaneously. Due attention must therefore be paid to the function of the archi-pattern in the overall hierarchy of the text, so that the signifier should not be subordinated to any signified.

The function of the archi-pattern in each separate drama will be examined with reference to one aspect central to the organisation of the text. In Ibsen it is the double plot structure; in O'Neill, the duologue; in Miller, the dramatic rhythm. In Albee, the discussion centres on the imaginary son as a metaphor for fictional self-conception; in Pinter, it centres on the function of the "micro-stories" in construction and deconstruction of family life, and in Shepard, homecoming is considered as part of a cyclic myth. The Conclusion will cluster the various strategies of the archi-pattern that have been observed, and trace the logic of the versions of the archi-pattern and their relationship to the socio-cultural code. Some formal aspects of the modern dramatic versions of the archi-pattern will then be considered. The conclusion will be that the prodigal son has become transmuted into a returning son, and that the emphasis has shifted from the son to the family to whom he returns: homecoming has become an ambiguous state.

II. THE HOMECOMING IN MODERN DRAMA

DOUBLE PLOT OF THE RETURNING SON AND DAUGHTER: *GHOSTS*

"Well, the son come home then"

Ghosts focuses on the problem of guilt as reflected in the characters' fidelity to "ghosts" of past people or attitudes. The drama revolves around the characters of Oswald and his mother. Both are bound to the "ghosts", he because of his inherited illness and she because her loyalty and conformity do not permit her to speak out.[1] Both wish to free themselves from the hold of the past on the present, though this requires that they confront the responsibility for the truth of their lives.

The dark secret from the recesses of the past is revealed as a result of the return of Oswald Alving, the "prodigal son", to his home.[2] A sub-plot, connected to the main plot, develops around a daughter, Regina Engestrand, who is searching for a home. Here too there is a secret, the daughter's origin, which is revealed towards the end of the play and is a crucial factor in her choice of a home. So this play is based on the retrospective method of a double plot, which centres on the links between generations, generational responsibility and individual responsibility, and the search for a homecoming in the broadest sense.[3]

The conflicting inner situation of the characters and their complex interrelationships, which originated in the past, are manifest in the dramatic structure of *Ghosts* as an analytic drama, one based on an

analysis of expired events, retrospective rather than prospective.[4]   The
events that precede those in the drama are revealed in expositions of the
past, which holds a dominant significance for everything that occurs later.
Typical of an analytical drama, the constant allusion to an event that
occurred in the past suggests a "secret" of which the characters are
unaware but ought — or would like — to know.[5] The secret cannot be
disclosed in the private domain, but has to be exposed in public.   This
secret, as is the case in *Ghosts,* is typically connected with justified or
imaginary feelings of guilt. In this play, the main dramatic function of the
secret is to motivate Mrs Alving's concealment of the past from those
affected by it (Oswald and Regina).

According to Levin, in the various modes of multiple-plot drama the
function of the comparative relations between the plots may vary. It may
be causal, so that "a character from one line of action directly affects the
other".[6]   In this play, the actions of the members of the Alving family
directly affect the Engstrand family; one can trace these influences
temporally, and compare the parallel stages of the plots.[7] Another mode
may be in evidence, as it is here: plots may be associated through
analogical relationships which develop spatially, so that "causation [is] not
produced by the action of cause-effect but by the analogy constructed
between them".[8] An examination of the two plots of *Ghosts* with regard
to both functions — the causal, which develops temporally, and the
analogical, which looks at the spatial relationships — highlights the place
of the prodigal son archi-pattern in this drama.

The relationship between the two plots, whether causal, analogical or
both, may be connected to other components in the strategy of the drama.
We therefore refer to Pavel's strategic "plot grammar" as well as to the
above-mentioned parallel plots according to Levin's theories.   "Plot
grammar", according to Pavel, is based on an analysis of "*Moves*" — their
essence and the relationships between them — with reference to three
strategic components: plot, characters and meaning. He describes these
as "the explicitness of plot advance, the role of character and groups of
characters, and the links between plot and meaning".[9] According to Pavel,
"An action is a *Move* if it either directly or indirectly brings about another

Move or if it ends the story".[10] Every *Move* is made by a character, who is motivated by a *Problem*. In itself, a *Move* constitutes an attempt to overcome the problem and reach a *Solution,* and is either assisted or inhibited by an event or another character, which serve as *Auxiliaries.*

We may suppose that in *Ghosts* a chain of narrative causality is created, motivated mainly by temporal external events as they affect the characters. But the organisation of the plot is also based on spatial analogy of elements, which illuminates aspects of the thematic composition.* Both these modes, the causal and the spatial, constitute components of the meanings of the two parallel plots. The causal mode focuses on the son's and daughter's *Moves*, the analogical mode on generational aspects; both of these relate to thematic aspects of the prodigal son archi-pattern.

The *Moves* of Oswald and Regina in the causal mode reveal how much the play is based on the search for a home. In Oswald's plot, this search is manifested in his longing to find a home as an answer and remedy for guilt feelings, a refuge from his fears and a source of help in assuaging his torment. In Regina's case, remaining where she is, leaving or returning to one "home" or another depends on how far her choice will advance her social status. Oswald is motivated to return home by his physical and mental state, while Regina's motives are linked to her social ambitions. This substantive difference between the two plots may be observed in an analysis of both characters' main *Moves*.

The structure of the Oswald plot shows the extent to which his *Problems* are internalized. The progress of his *Moves* shows a crescendo of internal intensity. There are hints of Oswald's guilt about his "joyous life" in Paris at the beginning of the play. His feelings about home are also internalized and ambiguous, as evident in his dialogue with Manders about the meaning of his return home (p. 113). It is unclear whether he is a "prodigal son" (i.e., coming home after a life of sin) or "the son come home" (i.e., simply a son returning home). Although the dialogue is antagonistic, Oswald agrees with Manders on one subject, at least: "A

---

*A chart of the *Moves* is included in the Notes

child's own home is, and always will be, his proper place" (p. 115). This uncharacteristic agreement on Oswald's part hints at the complexity of his attitude towards his home and, by extension, his mother. He resents having been sent away from home at an early age, and his associations with it are therefore somewhat negative. Yet his statement, "Oh, it's good to be home again" (p.115) underscores his longing for home as a refuge.

In the second act, the *Problem* of Oswald's mental anguish is intensified. The complexity of the *Problem* is expressed in the partial disclosure of the nature of his illness and the revelation of his feelings of guilt. He considers his way of life as having been the cause of this anguish, and this destroys him internally: "But all this torment — the regret, the remorse — and the deadly fear. Oh, this horrible fear!" (p.151). His helplessness in the face of his condition has deprived him of any satisfaction and joy of life, and has increased his longing for some other way of life that he has missed: "Oh! if only could live my life over again — if only I could undo what I have done" (p. 147).

In the third act his feelings of frustration and desperation grow stronger after he learns about his father's "secret", the disease he has inherited from him. The fire at the orphanage seems to him to reflect the collapse of his life: "Everything will be burnt up; nothing will be left that is in memory of my father. Here I am being burnt up, too" (p. 162). Regina's abandoning him to his fate brings his *Problem* to the final stage of desperation and his suffering closer to its end.

There is, then, an intensified, internalized sequence of helplessness and desperation on the part of Oswald, and his *Problem* is affected by external intervention only on two, late occasions in the play. The first is his mother's disclosure of the "secret", which takes place in the last act. In Oswald's eyes, his release from his sense of guilt and the transfer of the sin and blame onto his father are part of his liberation from the world of *Ghosts,* which demands that parents be treated with respect, according to outdated norms. He rejects these norms, labelling them "antiquated superstition" (p. 167). Although he does admit that the revelation of the secret has freed him from "remorse and self-reproach" (p. 168), he is still stricken by his horrible illness, which portends his death and leaves him deeply anxious that he will become "a helpless child again" (170). Regina's decision to leave the house, depriving him of her help, is the second and final time that Oswald's *Problems* are intensified, determined and executed by another character. Her leaving impels Oswald to turn to his mother as his last chance to ease his suffering, his final *Move*. Oswald's *Moves*, therefore, take place primarily within his inner world.

In contrast, Regina's *Problem* structure is more externalised. It stems from her aspirations for social advancement, and depends on the decisions of other characters in relation to her fate. In Act One, in her conversation with Engstrand, her behaviour and speech already underscore her ambition to change and advance her social position. This intention is revealed in her inept use of French phrases, her attitude towards "fine folk" (p. 95), and her contemptuous refusal to become part of her "father's" life. This initial situation is complicated when there seems to be some real chance of improving her social status. But this way out of her *Problem* is blocked when the secret of her birth and of Oswald's illness is revealed.

So her *Problem* structure is associated with social status rather than an inner personal situation like Oswald's, and its resolution is closely linked to the reactions of other characters. The disparity in the degree of centrality and internalisation of the dramatic presentation of the *Problems* of these two characters is also evident in the quantity of Oswald's dialogue, in which he lays bare his suffering. Regina, by contrast, makes rare appearances on stage and says little. She expresses her position in short, direct sentences, for example, her dialogue with Engstrand (Act One) and her reactions when the truth is revealed to her (Act Three). While these short speeches do not give a dimension of depth to her *Problems*, they make her pragmatic intentions abundantly clear.[11]

The differences in the structure of the two plots are also apparent in the nature of the *Auxiliaries* and *Solutions* associated with Oswald's and Regina's *Moves*. So the *Auxiliaries* and *Solutions* in the Oswald plot are linked to the other characters by mainly psychological elements, guilt, remorse and fear.[12] Only towards the end of the play do these relationships focus on physical succour. When the play opens Oswald has already returned to his home (*Move* 1); his return has been internally motivated and is a search for help in his wretched state, based on his inner faith that mother-home will provide him with shelter. This situation is developed dramatically by delaying the information regarding the reason for Oswald's return. Even in the scene in which he embraces Regina (*Move* 2), there is still no indication of how complicated and serious his condition really is.

In Act Two Oswald is encouraged by the *Auxiliary* of his mother's unconditional dedication to him, again, something which exists on an internal, affective level. Brought to despair by his condition, she asks, "My poor boy, how could I refuse you anything now?" (p. 149). He requests her consent to his liaison with Regina, which to him seems the only solution to his misfortune (*Move* 3). In his past flirtations with Regina, even before his final return home, and certainly now that his condition has taken a turn for the worse, he recognizes that "my salvation lay in her, for I saw the joy of life in her" (p. 152). The phrase "joy of life", which is repeated three times in his dialogue with his mother, expresses a psychological state.

In the third act, when his condition deteriorates, he looks not just for the "joy of life" but also for a helping hand from Regina, to help him end his life with dignity, an actual, physical *Solution* (*Move* 4). It is interesting that in this act Oswald no longer uses the phrase "joy of life". It becomes part of his mother's speech, an inner key for her to understand her husband's thirst for life.

We now proceed to *Move* 5 and his plea to his mother to bring about his speedy death, his final *Solutions*, now an external one: "I never asked you for life...you shall take it back" (p. 171).[13] The Oswald *Move*-plot and all its associated aspects finally focus on the son's unequivocal and final return to his home, akin to a fetal return to his mother's womb, to the dust of the earth. Oswald needs a home, which his mother is ready to give him, in which he will be received "like a helpless child again" (p. 170). Mrs Alving replies "My child has his mother to tend him" (p. 170). The

Moves, *Problems*, *Auxiliaries* and *Solutions* of Oswald's plot, then, are centered on the themes of guilt, responsibility, deterioration and return, and they form a primarily symbolic, internalized sequence.

Regina's search for a home, in contrast, is driven by her ambition for social advancement. She has a number of choices of "homes" to live in or return to, but all of them are dependent on the desires of other characters. She has four possible options: Mrs Alving's home (and the orphanage where she is supposed to work); Engestrand's "Sailors' Home"; the home of Pastor Manders; or marriage with Oswald and a home in Paris. All these options are apparent at the beginning of the play, portrayed with varying degrees of explicitness (the *Solutions* of *Move* 1 and *Move* 2).

In her dialogue with Engestrand, she states emphatically that she will not return to her father and his Sailors' Home as a substitute for her status with the Alvings: "Do you suppose I am going home with you? To such a house as yours? Not likely" (p. 97). Her inept use of French phrases and her concern for Oswald's welfare also hint at her expectation of a better future if she were to throw her lot in with Oswald. In her conversation with Manders, she more than hints that she is "capable and willing" of easing Oswald's loneliness. Of all these choices, he is her best opportunity — *Move* 2.

In the second act (*Move* 3), when she is persuaded to join the masters of the house in a champagne toast, her hesitation shows her social ambitions as well as her inferior position in the household. When Manders expresses his astonishment at her new-found status, she betrays her lack of confidence: "It is not my fault, Mr Manders" (p. 155). Nonetheless, she consents to Oswald's request that she join him in Paris (*Solution*, *Move* 3). In Act Three she is promised her long-sought home with Oswald, but it involves caring for him; now, in her own words, she has inherited the "joy of life" from her mother and refuses to go with him. In her final decision to leave the Alving home (*Move* 4) she throws in her lot with the other two houses which are left as her last chance of finding a home. Her idea of finding a place with the pastor — "Mr Manders takes an interest in me, I know" (p. 166) — is not taken up by him, though he seems tempted. She also has the possibility of the "Alving House", the Sailors Home.

To summarise, the main plot is motivated mainly internally, the sub-plot externally. Neither shows a real dynamic of change in the nature of the *Problems*, rather, the situation sketched out at the beginning of the play intensifies over its course. *Moves*, *Problems*, *Auxiliaries* and *Solutions* bear out this internal/external continuum.

The comparison of the main plot and the sub-plot in Levin's other mode, the analogical, or spatial, reveals a pattern of relationships between generations. The analogies between actions and events linked to the past and the present, the generation of fathers, mothers, the sons and daughters, will be analysed in terms of some familiar thematic aspects of the archi-pattern: guilt/innocence (concerning "truth"), inward/outward (return to "home"), and life/death.

As stated, the main plot focuses on the effort to separate the "truth" of what has happened in the past from the "ghosts" and the guilt they create. These are the "ghosts of beliefs" according to which the parents and the children have conducted their lives. There is a tension between these beliefs and the living truth which makes it possible to feel "the joy of life", and it is the truth which parents and children either search for or bury, in both plots.[14] The "ghosts" of two dead parents, Alving and Joanna, are also very much present in the play. The return of the prodigal son becomes a catalyst for soul-searching (in the main plot) and for a better place to live (in the sub-plot). The soul-searching for 'truth' is constantly interpreted by another 'parent'-character.

The parent generation — Mrs Alving and Engstrand — includes an additional character, Pastor Manders. His reactions emphasise the underlying irony about what is considered "truth" in the eyes of the older generation. Manders' behaviour and speeches cast light on the hypocrisy of the familial relationships, emphasising the space between the mendacious "ghosts" and the truth which hides behind them. His comments about the values and moral preferences of the parent figures serve an ironic function, pointing up the "ghostly" character of the choices made.[15] His attitude towards "truth" as expressed in his dialogues with Mrs Alving and with Engstrand, epitomises the moral attitudes of the main parent characters in both plots. Because he himself submits so completely to public opinion, he insures all of his own property but does not insure the public orphanage, lest someone suspect him of not relying entirely on God. He is apprehensive about public reaction to a woman being in a strange man's house (Mrs Alving in his home or the possibility of his spending the night in her home), but tries to persuade Regina to live in Engstrand's house even after he learns that the latter is not her father. In his dialogue with Oswald about the life of artists in Paris, he denounces "open immorality", but is ready to reconcile himself to whatever happens in the privacy of the home.

The exposition of the events which occurred before the dramatic present recalls the guilt/innocence theme of the archi-pattern, and this theme further informs much of the course of the play. The difference between the plots lies in the degree of awareness and regret regarding the circumstances of the marriages of the parent generation. The analogy between the parent couples in each plot is based on concealment of the truth about the two spouses, who according to the hypocritical Manders were a "fallen man" and a "fallen woman".[16]

Mrs Alving and Engstrand both relate the education and rearing of the younger generation to money from the sinning parent's past. Mrs Alving insists that her son will never inherit his father's wealth: "My son shall have everything from me. I am determined" (p. 125).[17] Engstrand, in his deceitful way, claims that every cent he received from the "American" went to pay for his daughter's education and that he "can give a faithful account of every single penny of it" (p. 140). Pastor Manders falls into the snare of pretence and flattery that the carpenter lays for him, and accepts Engstrand's version of his marriage and his rearing of Regina. His conclusion is "how exceedingly careful we ought to be in condemning our fellow man" (p. 142).

Mrs Alving and Engstrand both have a "secret", a sign of the guilt/innocence thematic aspect. They both hide the sins of their spouses from their children and society as a whole, but their attitudes differ. Mrs Alving acknowledges her guilt: she achieves awareness of the fact that she acted as she did because she was a "coward" and gave in to the accepted rules of "law and order" without really understanding her husband's predicament. She was also guilty of hiding the truth from her son and ruining her own life. Engstrand, who does not know the whole truth about the sins of his former wife, continues to try and conceal what he does know from Regina, who is supposedly his daughter. He self-righteously protests that everything he did was for Joanna's good: "that was how I rescued her and made her my lawful wife, so that no one should know how recklessly she had carried on with a stranger" (p. 139).

Mrs Alving and Engstrand both turn to acts of philanthropy to atone for the sins of their spouses or to appear charitable. Mrs Alving claims "the orphanage is to exist, to silence all rumours and clear away all doubts" (p. 125). Engstrand wants to establish a Sailors' Home with "honest money" (p. 141). Analogous to the orphanage, and obviously an ironic version of it, this will be sort of refuge: "in this house of mine they should have a sort of parental care looking after them".

The incident of the fire in the orphanage and the financial and spiritual support given to the Sailors' Home in its wake again underscore the differences between the two plots, despite their outward similarity. While Mrs Alving finally realises that "the orphanage would never have come to any good" (p. 159), Engstrand is capable of extorting the means to establish his home from Manders. The self-righteous pose Engstrand assumes in establishing a home purportedly for the public good reaches an ironic peak when he declares it will be called the "Alving Home".[18] Manders joins Engstrand, even indicating his readiness to help materially, in these enterprise.

The speeches of both Mrs Alving and of Engstrand are laced with expressions of guilt, remorse and the longing for atonement. But these similar feelings differ greatly in their depth and sincerity.[19] Mrs Alving views her past behaviour as having shown her as "too much of a coward" (p. 131). She adopts a different standard for her behaviour and now views her life in terms of "if I had been the woman I ought to be" (p. 131). She is able to recognize the frustrations her husband encountered were to a great extent because she "brought no holiday spirit into his home" (p. 164). Throughout the unfolding of the plot, she gains greater insight and a deeper awareness. Although she still tries, as she always has, to keep the situation under control, she is finally forced to resign herself and accept the tragic role of a mother who must make the choice between taking the life of her son, who in any case is doomed, or to prolong his agony.[20]

Engstrand, on the other hand, although he feigns remorse and pretends to take responsibility for the errors of his ways, is being patently deceitful when he says, "Heaven have mercy on me as a sinner! My conscience isn't worth our speaking about, Pastor Manders" (p.131). In the presence of the pastor and Mrs Alving, his speech is sprinkled with Scriptural references: "erring mortal" (p.110), "price of your sin" (p. 148), "angel of salvation" (p. 160), among others. After the fire, hiding behind these seemingly pious expressions, he attaches blame for it to Manders and threatens him with public disclosure. He extorts benefits for himself under the guise of a sacrificial victim: "I know someone who has taken the blame for someone else on his shoulders before now, I do" (p. 161).[21]

Manders, for whom the sincerity of guilt and remorse are less important than how these traits look in public, again falls into the trap of flattery.[22] He appears prepared to forgive any sin, any guilt, which does not have a public aspect. In his view, "One certainly is not called upon to account to everyone for what one reads or thinks in the privacy of one's own home" (p. 103).

The second thematic aspect of the prodigal son archi-pattern, that of inward/outward, is directly linked in *Ghosts* to the third, that of life/death. Oswald's act of leaving home, wandering in foreign lands, his material and/or moral degradation — all arouse a sense of death-like loss and abandonment, and stand in contrast to life-giving remorse and the return home, at least for a time. The inward/outward pattern in the Oswald plot, like the motivation for his *Moves*, is primarily subjective. His return may be like that of the prodigal son, as he himself indicates, but he is about to become lost again, this time in the finality of oblivion.

Regina was "lost" but was retrieved and returned "home" by Mrs Alving, without knowing the cause for this and without any regard for her own feelings. Once her origin is disclosed and her parents are blamed for their "fault" (not the "guilt" of the main plot), she leaves the Alving home of her own volition to seek another "home". This is equated in moral terms with her becoming "lost" again: as Mrs Alving puts it, "Regina...you are going to your ruin" (p. 166).

Manders, in his Janus-like moral judgement, preaches on the norms of leaving and returning home. He is instrumental in persuading Regina that she must return to her father's home, but hints at his own willingness to help her, suggesting that she lodge with him. He is also the one who gives expression to the connection between the "sin" of leaving and the meaning of return in the Oswald plot, interpreting Oswald's life in Paris as being "lost".[23]

We may conclude that the structure of the two plots and their interconnection, whether by the sequence of causal events pointing to the son's/daughter's search for home or analogies which can be drawn spatially about the generational sphere, are meaningfully linked to thematic aspects of the prodigal son archi-pattern. They also relate markedly in terms of some plot segments.

The "secret", that sets Oswald's and Regina's returning and leaving in motion is unknown at the start of the play. It is revealed to them during its course, but each perceives it differently. In Oswald's case the secret releases him from his guilt, but at the same time heightens his fears. For Regina, the knowledge of her parents' identities neither resolves nor awakens guilt feelings, but only provides her with an opportunity to demand her share of the inheritance, and augments her efforts to find the home where she will do best.

But it is Manders who alludes directly to segments of the archi-pattern. He blames Mrs Alving for having allowed "your son to wander so long" (p. 107); he expresses his doubts about whether Oswald has managed to "keep the inner man free from harm" in Paris.

The narrative segment of "recognition" may also be found in *Ghosts*. Oswald ironically tries (and succeeds in) exposing Manders' recognition of him as hypocrisy. Mrs Alving raises doubts when she says "if you recognize him again" (p. 105), and Manders "thought for a moment it was his father in the flesh" (p. 114), conjuring up the ghost of Captain Alving.

Yet the single mention of the "prodigal son" as such belongs to Oswald:

> Manders: I — I — no, can it possibly be -?
> Oswald: Yes, it really is the prodigal son, Mr Manders.
> Manders: Oh, my dear young friend —
> Oswald: Well, the son come home then (p. 113).

This dialogue cannot be anything but ironic. Oswald is simply anticipating what he knows Manders will think of him. However, he is plagued by guilt, which during the play is removed from his shoulders and transferred to his sinful father. Oswald becomes the returning son, who longs to find in his home a cure for both his physical and mental affliction.

DUOLOGUE BETWEEN FATHER, SON AND BROTHERS:
LONG DAY'S JOURNEY INTO NIGHT

"[who] will always be a stranger
who never feels at home"

Christianity and the parables of the Bible had a strong impact on O'Neill's writing, and in the mid-thirties this influence grew even greater. In *Long Day's Journey into Night* the prodigal son plays a central role, both thematically and as an element in the dramatic structure.[1]

E. Tornquist claims that scholars have only recently become aware of the extent to which O'Neill's writing "is permeated with religious allusions and symbols". He cites as an example the one-act play *The Rope* (1918) which "is patterned rather closely to the parable of the prodigal son in the New Testament and somehow less closely to the episode concerning Esau's birthright in the old one".[2]

G.Y. Williams, in his analysis of the background to *The Dreamy Kid* (1918), centres on the return of the play's prodigal grandson to his dying grandmother's bed and its echo of O'Neill's family experiences, at a time when he and his brother Jamie regarded themselves as prodigals. Williams states that: "The prodigal son parable could not have been far from O'Neill's mind that year, early and late".[3] He also points to the parable of the prodigal son in *The Rope*, in which the son Luke returns to his elderly father's New England farm. A similar combination of the family

backdrop and the interwoven motif of the prodigal son are particularly
evident in the later play, *Long Day's Journey Into Night*.

Many studies have been conducted on the influence of O'Neill's life on
his plays, all of which stress his fixation on his family. These
autobiographical materials are evident throughout the body of his work,
giving expression to his memories of his mother's drug addiction and
death, his brother's existential fear and dependence on alcohol, his father's
loss of dignity and disappointments as an actor and his own complex
relationship with his family, along with the uncertainties and torments
which affected his entire life.[4] Hence one can understand the dominance
of the confessional urge in his work: "... so much of O'Neill's work derives
from his compulsion to confess, to focus on his haunting memories even
as he was ashamed to acknowledge them".[5] This autobiographical element
is reflected, and even transcended, in *Long Day's Journey into Night,*
which is both his personal confessional and his finest dramatic
achievement.

Emotions linked to past memories and their impact on the present, the
drive to achieve self-awareness as well as knowledge of others are shared
by all the characters in the play. The "journey" that goes on into the small
hours of the night is one into the depths of the pasts of each of the four
family members in the present. Their desperate and unsuccessful attempts
to listen to one another form the basis for the dialogue which characterizes
this play. The recoil movement of the dialogues towards the past, and their
expressive and appellative nature in relation to the present inner world of
the characters contain variations on the thematic horizon of the prodigal
son.[6]

As well as the fact of Edmund's return, other parallels may be drawn
with the Ur-scene. These are particularly evident if we consider the
dialogues of Act Four. These will be analysed at a later stage; for the
moment, it is sufficient to note that the Ur-scene also has the pattern of
son/father followed by brother/brother. Guilt, return and death —
thematic aspects of the archi-pattern — inform the play, and there is a step

onward from Ibsen with regard to the plot segment of the "secret", which is known here, but ignored.

Edmund returns to his home, like Oswald, in search of protective and redemptive shelter, but also out of a longing for home as a state of being.[7] His return arouses a compulsive desire for renewed self-recognition in the other family members, as well as their exposing themselves to others in order to gain an understanding of the truth of their lives. The process of self-knowledge includes a stage of recognition of guilt, and indeed "guilt" is the most dominant word in the text.[8] The family members, alternately talking about their own guilt and the guilt of others, arouse feelings of repentance and self-abnegation. Mary is caught between love for her family and her accusations against them. She blames her husband for making her give up plans to become a nun or a concert pianist, and for thwarting her desire to make a home for her family. She blames Jamie, her eldest, for the death of the infant Eugene. The birth of her younger son, Edmund, is linked to the beginning of her drug addiction, as well as to sense of guilt that he may have inherited his illness from her consumptive father. Tyrone blames his parents for the course his life has taken, envies his sons the love of their mother, and complains bitterly of the whole family's extravagance that is likely to land him in the poorhouse. He himself stands as self-accused and blamed by his family for his stinginess, which they think caused Mary's and Edmund's condition; at least he did nothing to help them. Jamie claims his father is to blame for his mother's drug addiction and the neglect of his brother's illness. He bears a grudge against his brother Edmund, whose birth led to the mother's drug addiction and deprived him of his parents' love.

The returning son, Edmund, levels the fewest accusations against the others.[9] Still, from time to time he gives vent to his deep resentment of his father's stinginess, which is apt to impair his chances of recovery. He pleas for his mother's attention, appealing to her to recognize his poor health and to show him some love. He is the most willing to forgive, out of a sense of empathy with others which leads him even to forget his own condition. He is ready to relinquish his own desires for the sake of their needs and wishes. In the last act, he tends to become more active, to come between

Tyrone and Jamie, as well as protecting his mother from the latter's accusations.

The complexity and duality of the human soul is one of O'Neill's tenets. It is revealed in this play through the relationships between the father and sons, and is particularly evident in the relationships between the brothers. As several critics have pointed out, this conviction is reflected throughout the dramatist's canon, whether in paired characters (often brothers) who seem like two sides of the same individual, or in single brothers whose conflicting actions betoken divided feelings and desires. This complexity of generational and sibling relationships is reminiscent of the archi-pattern.

The element linked to the depths of the past in this drama does not necessarily lie in a "secret" concerning a specific event or person. The mother's addiction to drugs, as well as Tyrone's, Edmund's and Jamie's addiction to alcohol, are well known to all the characters. This knowledge is repressed on the basis of hopes that arise from their decisions to rid themselves of their addictions, which are the opening point of the play. Jamie's growing awareness of his mother's addiction forces him to resign himself completely to his own fate, but has no real influence on the way Tyrone and Edmund live their lives. Edmund returns to the family home at a time of some hope (Mary's short-lived, illusory rehabilitation, an unawareness of the severity of Edmund's illness). When he returns these illusions are shattered, and the past once again bursts into the present. The element of the past functions mainly in the way the characters relate to it and how far they attribute their failure to it.[10] Its significance does not lie in an external occurrence, nor does it depend on the interest evinced in it by one of the other characters. Rather, the past is important owing to an internal pressure, relentlessly compelling the characters to tell the others their version of the past and its effect on their present condition.[11] This process is revealed in the dialogues.

As A. Kennedy comments:

> "The final act of *Long Day's Journey Into Night* is constructed to elicit — or
> provoke — just such a series of intimate confessions in two long duologues.
> That structuring around duologues is itself remarkable, for O'Neill has
> considerable skill in creating group dialogue".[12]

Thus, to examine more intensively the existence of the prodigal son
thematic horizon, as well as any digressions from it, we must turn to the
central dialogues in the final act of the play.[13] These are constructed as
confessional duologues.[14] The first occurs between the father and
Edmund, and the second between Jamie and Edmund. Both the contents
and the sequence of the two duologues evoke the structure of the Ur-scene,
which also contains two duologues, one between the father and the
returning son, and another between the older brother and his father, and
relates to the relationships between the brothers and their father. The link
to the Ur-Scene is further highlighted by allusions in the play to the Bible
and the New Testament. Expressions like "Jesus", "study of the Bible",
"Christ", "Christian act", "deny God", "last judgement", "go to hell",
"saved", "God is my judge", and so on, recur constantly throughout the
whole play, particularly in the duologues. Although these expressions may
be viewed as a reflection of the playwright's religious faith, the frequency
of their appearance in this play seems to link them to the Ur-scene.

The element of constant disclosure to others is the basis for the
duologues. This confessional mood characterizes the first duologue and is
interwoven into Jamie's speech in his duologue with Edmund. It is
particularly marked in Jamie's statement that he feels as if he had "gone
to confession" (p. 147). The confessional duologue has another significant
trait. It is always linked to and framed by a situation loaded with past
events, relating explicitly or implicitly to a third character, and is marked
by a struggle within the character or between the two characters either to
ignore the confessional situation or to recognize it and accept responsibility
for it.[15] In this way, these confessional duologues are to a great extent
situation-bound. In other words, there is a very close connection between
speech, action and situation.[16] In this play the actual placement of these
central duologues emphasises their being situation-bound: they come

between the two episodes which centre on the mother.[17] At the end of Act Three, Mary's appearance and speech show that she is still in touch with reality, but when she reappears at the end of the play, after the two duologues, she is entirely cut off from events. Thus the two duologues function within the frame of the disintegration of the mother's personality and its effect on the course of the characters' lives. This element is theatrically highlighted by the fact that all the way through the duologues, the mother's steps can be heard as she paces, drugged, in her room above, as if she were haunting the speakers below: "Yes. She'll be nothing but a ghost haunting the past by this time" (p. 133). Her withdrawal into fantasy permits the revealing confessions among the other members of the family, but at the same time she is never out of their thoughts and she forms the painful backdrop to their words.[18]

These duologues have a special stylistic nature expressed mainly in the sharp transitions between the lines and the interrupted sentences. There are several reasons for these devices: the repression of subjects which are taboo, the fear of an emotional outburst from the speaker or those listening in connection with a certain subject, the desire of one of the participants to support the other. As a result of this situation, each of the two duologues has a three-part structure, the rhythm between each part forming an aspect of the special character of the confessional duologue: "appeal", "presentation of self" and "revelation".

In the first stage, which we term the "appeal" stage, as it is characterized by a request for confirmation, each of the participants makes an effort to turn a more receptive ear toward the character with whom he is talking. Although accusing the other, he also tries to justify his own behaviour to himself and the other. He still attempts to repress his own strong impulse to confess, but at the same time wishes to make his agonized confession so that he may gain the understanding and support of the other. Because of these opposing drives, the pace of the duologue is rapid, expressed in frequently alternating speakers, interrupted sentences, and sharp transitions from one subject to another.[19] The jumps from subject to subject suggest, like a sub-text, the vacillations of the psyche from guilt to self-justification, thus preparing the ground for the next two stages.

The second stage is "presentation of self", in which the character leading the duologue presents himself and his situation, basing himself mainly on a repressed knowledge of past events and their effect on the present. On this level, the character tries to excuse and justify his own behaviour, and by attributing the reasons for it to the past, asks for the listener's understanding and forgiveness. The speaker still has control over his repressed emotions to a certain degree, and tries to represent his behaviour in a positive and rational light. At this stage, the segments of duologue are longer, interrupted by the listener's reactions, as the speaker tries to understand his expressed or mute arguments and doubts, and to respond to them.

The third stage in the sequence of confessional duologue is "revelations", in which the speaker is swept along by his emotions, and his words reveal his inner truth. Often he is aware that he is hurting the other person, but at other times will ignore his very existence. The active nature of this stage is expressed by the speaker's breaking away from reality, and at the end of the duologue he has some difficulty returning to it.

This division is schematic, and in fact each stage contains some aspects of the next. This creates the flowing rhythm of the confession as evident in the two duologues discussed here.

In the "appeal" stage of the duologue between Tyrone and Edmund (from the beginning of the act until the story of Tyrone's past), they accuse one another, but also search for communication and understanding. The tone is set when Edmund enters and his father receives him with the words, "I'm glad you've come, lad. I've been damned lonely" (p. 109). They keep reaching out for an attentive ear and sympathy while expressing their love and support for each other.[20] This may be sensed even as they tease each other over who can down the most alcohol, bicker about saving electricity, gossip about Jamie's preferred pastimes, or argue about who was the greater genius, Shakespeare or one of Edmund's favourite poets.

Their conversation about each of these topics evokes the bitter taste of self and mutual blame. The subject of drunkenness calls to mind Edmund's poor health, while the question of saving on electricity relates to Tyrone's stinginess and its effect on the family. When Tyrone accuses Jamie of being a loafer, and he and Edmund argue about their taste in authors, this underscores both Edmund's illness and Tyrone's failure as a Shakespearean actor. However, throughout all of the arguments and counter-arguments in this duologue, the antagonism is tinged with their desire to communicate with one another. It is this drive for mutual understanding and the desire to alleviate the sense of guilt that leads Tyrone to present his description of Mary's father, portraying him as an alcoholic consumptive, and contradicting the picture previously drawn by Mary. Similarly, he belittles Mary herself. Tyrone hopes to gain Edmund's understanding and sympathy by these revelations, thereby mitigating his responsibility for Mary's deteriorating condition. While there are in this duologue expressions of pain, guilt feelings and accusation, these are all motivated by love, and the desire to justify oneself to others.[21] They both try to avoid painful subjects and to ignore Mary's footsteps which they hear from the room above. "We know that we're trying to forget" (p. 114). The inner rush of passions, alternating between feelings of guilt, accusation and a desire for forgiveness, is apparent in every expression: for example, when the father says of Edmund "it's a case of a poor thing but mine own" (p. 124), or "I can't help liking you, in spite of everything" (ibid.).

The second stage of the duologue, the "presentation of self", is where Tyrone, focusing on his memories, blames his father for abandoning the family, returning to England and committing suicide, leaving him, a young boy, as the family breadwinner. At the age of ten he was "the man of the family" (p. 129), bearing the burden of saving his family and himself from the poorhouse. By bringing up these memories, Tyrone hopes to justify his present behaviour as rooted in the past and beyond his control. His words, "Yes, maybe life overdid the lesson for me" (p. 130), are a typical expression of this attempt at self-justification.

From this point on, the confessional duologue moves to the "revelation" stage. Here Tyrone reveals that he gave up the chance of being a Shakespearean actor for the career of a popular actor, in order to be a big moneymaker. Although at this stage too the speaker returns to events of the past, the stress is on his present feelings. The affective aspect and the existential pain over a "life that was not lived" overcome the real or imagined hardships in the everyday struggle for existence. The external reasons for having chosen the course of life that led to the present situation are no longer even mentioned, since they are superseded by the pain of the situation. "What the hell was it I wanted to buy, I wonder, that was worth — well, no matter. It's a late day for regrets" (p. 132). Tyrone knows that by making this revelation he may have repelled Edmund, but in stating this knowledge he seems to be asking Edmund to deny it.[22] "Maybe I shouldn't have told you. Maybe you'll only feel contempt for me".

Edmund's part in the duologue is more dispersed, and inserted in the gaps between Tyrone's long speeches. In his life, as in the theatre, Tyrone wants the stage to himself, and dominates the conversation. It is perhaps because of this that Edmund's own appeal stage takes place in almost complete compliance with his father's attempt to win him over. In his presentation stage, however, there is a certain holding back from the depths of the ego. Edmund retreats into symbolism, particularly with regard to the triple metaphor of fog/sea/ghost as "three Gorgons in one". His digression here alludes to the illusion of self-knowledge: "As if I was a ghost belonging to the fog, and the fog was the ghost of the sea" (p. 113). In the revelation segment, he repeats these elements of fog/sea/ghost, but describes the experience of the passing moment as a metaphysical experience: "For a second you see — and seeing the secret are the secret". His experience here transcends time and takes on an archetypal cyclic meaning in which the moment of death and the descent into the sea is also the moment of rebirth.[23] Edmund is therefore without past or future in the dimensions of time, and feels he is someone "who never feels at home" (p. 135) in the dimensions of place. He experiences a longing to drown in the sea (in his mother) — the death of a man who throughout his life "must always be a little in love with death!" (p. 135). His revelation is marked by the difficulty he finds in expressing his predicament; his tendency to sink into the depths of his soul makes the return to reality hard for him. In his search for a fitting expression as a man and an author, Edmund knows that at least he can say about his own words, "Well, it will be a faithful realism, at least" (ibid.). He senses that he has in him "the making of a poet", but he is only capable of coming up with something that fits the statement, "stammering is the native eloquence of us fog people".[24]

Edmund, the returning son, is a sort of ghost within a ghost, who struggles to gain an understanding of the meaning of life. At the same time, however, he knows he must adjust to stark reality even if this means going on living like a ghost. His return is like coming back from a fog, akin to a mystical experience, to a house shrouded in fog, isolated from the world, its occupants making a painful journey into the innermost recesses of their souls.

The two partners in the duologue, the returning son and his father, undergo a process of ever-growing search and avoidance of the truth. The difference in content between the process of each of these two experiences lies in their disparate value orientation. All three parts of Tyrone's speech relate to role achievement and moneymaking. Even at the end of the confession stage, he returns to the norms he has always held when he says, "And it's a poor way to convince you of the value of a dollar" (p. 132). In contrast, Edmund's system of values is oriented towards a search for an existential experience which is transcendent in nature.[25]

In the second duologue, between Edmund and Jamie, a noticeable difference in the balance of the partnership occurs. Edmund, perhaps under the influence of the preceding duologue, says very little: Jamie is the dominant speaker. Edmund, characteristically, is the "pardoner" here, only bursting out when his love for his mother is aroused (p. 142). The emphasis in the second duologue is squarely on Jamie.

Jamie reveals himself to a profound and painful degree, and his confession is to a growing extent situation-bound.[26] In it, Jamie also passes through the rhythm of all three stages: appeal, presentation of self and revelation. In the first of these, Jamie turns to his kid brother, expressing his love for him. Looking for a platform from which to launch a dialogue, he brings up subjects they used to talk about in the past: their father's stinginess, their mother's illness and "suitable feminine companionship" (p. 139). Jamie makes a cynical remark about his drunkenness, since this is the normal state of affairs and no surprise to either of them: "Unnecessary information Number One, eh?" (p. 136). When the urge for self-revelation intensifies, he reaches out for his brother's understanding and sympathy: "We've been more than brothers. You're the only pal I've ever had. I love your guts. I'd do anything for you" (p. 143).

In the presentation stage, he defends himself against something on the very edge of his consciousness. He accuses Edmund of thinking he wants to get the family property, and boasts of his superiority to his brother, claiming he is the one who shaped his personality: "I made you! You're my Frankenstein!" (p. 144). From this point onwards, he becomes increasingly caught up in the whirlpool of feelings of jealousy, hate, love and concern which he reveals. While in the first part of the presentation the process of confession was linked to envy mainly of external elements (property and preparing his brother for life), in the transition to the revelation stage the confession tends to spill over to inner feelings. Jamie warns Edmund of a destructive jealousy in both the past and the present, which could manifest itself as a real danger in the future. Above all: "Wanted you to fail. Always jealous of you. Mama's baby, Papa's pet!" (p. 146). The revenge he cautions Edmund about is mingled not only with feelings of self-blame but also of pity for the other. This part of the duologue is devoted entirely to an outburst of profound emotions which are not necessarily linked to any activity or to any particular situation or time.

We can now sum up those aspects in which O'Neill's play resembles the two parts of the Ur-scene of the New Testament. We have already noted one basic similarity, the sequence of the two duologues, of son/father and brother/brother. In the two duologues, as in the entire play, a sense of guilt predominates. Here, however, the accent moves from the sons to the parents (Mary, Tyrone and their parents). The returning son re-awakens and deepens the awareness of guilt. However, unlike the Ur-scene, he, not the father (and mother), is the one who is capable of forgiving and understanding.

In the duologue between the brothers there are also some echoes of the motif of "the dead", which appears in the Ur-scene. Jamie likens his condition to that of a dead man, and suggests that Edmund think of him in that way: "I had a brother, but he's dead" (p. 147). He warns his brother to look out for him when he comes back (from the sanatorium), saying he'll "be waiting to welcome" him (p. 147), only to send him back to the world of the dead.

In Jamie's personality there is a part which has "died" in his confrontation with reality, which impels him to forget his failed life by constantly losing himself in a fog of alcohol. His frustration at the sight of his mother's deteriorating condition, following upon his illusory hopes for her recovery, plunges him into a well of self-pity which he pathetically projects onto Fat Violet. In the duologue with his brother, he reveals his tangled emotions, a blend of love and hate, that suppressed part which has died within him. His love for, dependence on, envy of and hate for his brother are all expressed here. His confession about his past efforts to "prepare" Edmund for real life by introducing him to the world turns out to be ambiguous, when he admits he did it only to make Edmund fail. But the very fact of his confession reinforces his love for Edmund, his kid brother.   As many critics have pointed out, Jamie has certain Mephistophelean qualities.   Others have noted the impact of another Biblical story, Cain and his jealousy towards Abel.[27]

In the duologue between the brothers the topic of jealousy is intensified and pertains, as in the Ur-scene, to property as well as to the favouritism of the parents. The returning son and his older brother (referred to as "the absent brother", an epithet recalling the lost prodigal), feel like strangers not only in the world but to each other. They both search for ways to determine their self-identity, to prove themselves and to break free of their guilt feelings and their dependence on others.   But on the long and seemingly endless journey into night, each gropes to find his way, alternately pushing the other away and pulling him back.

Within the brothers' duologue, which is so powerful and revealing, Jamie's character, that of a man in conflict with himself and everyone else, is the dominant one. Research on the play has shown that O'Neill made major changes in his final version, in an attempt to weaken the personality of the elder brother in relation to the younger one. In O'Neill's words: "'Journey' is about the Tyrone family, and while Jamie is a necessary piece in the family puzzle, he cannot be allowed to overshadow his kin, particularly his younger brother Edmund".[28]   Critics, as well as directors and actors, have long puzzled over how best theatrically to interpret the characters, and who should overshadow whom.   Reflecting on the brother's envy in the Ur-scene, one may say that the tension of competition and jealousy between the returning brother and the younger brother also existed in the writing and production of the play.

In *Long Day's Journey Into Night,* as in *Ghosts,* the characters constantly grope after the "truth", a search reflected in *Ghosts* by Mrs Alving's and Oswald's feelings of guilt.   The "truth" and its opposite, which is expressed as "duty" and "dead beliefs" in Ibsen, and as a "lie" in O'Neill, is akin to ghosts in both plays.   However, in the former, these ghosts are rooted in social hypocrisy which must be cast off, while in the latter they are the result of internalization of illusions, which can only be dispelled by a painful, yet necessary, process.[29] To O'Neill, a play is "life in terms of lives".[30]

O'Neill wrote in the programme notes for the Provincetown Playhouse production:

> [Naturalism] represents our Father's daring aspiration towards self recognition by holding the family Kodak up to ill nature. But to us their old audacity is blague [sic]; we have taken too many snapshots of each other in every graceless position; we have endured too much from the banality of surfaces.[31]

We have seen a transition from Ibsen, marked in the move from primarily external values to an internalized exploration of the self within the context of a family that is not as safe as it looks. As in Ibsen, however, the family, the return to it and the life within it, which was supposed to be a haven of safety, a source of identity and warm and supportive relationships, turns out to be nothing more than an elusive, though necessary, ideal. The characters' quest for it leads them, through much soul searching, to seek an identity valid in their own eyes and in the eyes of others.

RHYTHM BETWEEN FATHERS AND SONS:
DEATH OF A SALESMAN

"The Inside of his Head"

The returning son in *Death of a Salesman* is Biff, who left home and became a "one dollar man". His return home, not, we note, for the first time, intensifies a continuous family crisis focusing on Willy, the father, as the protagonist of the play. Homecoming and its effects are a recurrent situation, and the final homecoming is dramatized as the climax of a lengthy, complicated inner process. The deep and disturbing relationship between father and returning son is doubled with another meaningful father-son relationship, between Willy as a son and the father figure to whom he relates affectively. The relationship between Biff and his father revolves around misunderstanding and "guilt"; that between Willy and his father takes place wholly in the realm of fantasy. There is a similar doubling of brother relationships: the ambiguous relationship between Biff and Happy and the tie between Willy and his brother Ben in the former's fantasy world. In both relationships, the son who left arouses envy in the son who stayed. This double set of father/son and brother/brother relationships emphasises the aspects of the archi-pattern in this drama, and the effect is achieved by focusing on Willy's inner life. This inner life is peopled by characters who are effectively a "cast of ideals".

At his father's grave Biff sums up Willy's life thus: "He had the wrong dreams. All, all wrong" (p.222). Biff, in his belated understanding of his father, recognizes Willy's dreamlike ideals but regards them as false. Miller himself explained:

> The trouble with Willy Loman is that he has tremendously powerful ideals...
> ... [the play's aim is] to set forth what happens when a man does not have a grip
> on the forces of life and has no sense of values which will lead him to that kind
> of a grip.[1]

This statement by the playwright emphasises the gap between adherence to ideals and the ability to function successfully in real life.

Biff is the only character in the play who understands the importance of Willy's inability to find the "right dream", and that his life was, for him, a torment. It is to Biff, the returning son, to whom Willy relates most affectively. The function of the returning son is linked to the father's value-orientation and ideals, which are both embodied in his fantasy, his memories, and his expectations of himself and of others. Willy not only tries, albeit unsuccessfully, to live up to his own moral code, he also judges everyone around him by that code. It is most painful to him to see Biff falling short of his ideals. Biff's reappearance evokes Willy's reminiscences as well as his self-expectations as son, brother and father. The subtitle of *Death of a Salesman, Certain Private Conversations in Two Acts and a Requiem,* as well as the title originally considered by the playwright, *The Inside of His Head,* already point to the play's thematic essence and major formal characteristic.[2] Thematically, Miller's drama deals with the tension between the protagonist's private inner world and external reality. Its principal structural characteristic consists of the integration of dramatic realism and expressionism.[3]

The conflicting inner selves that make up Willy Loman's many-sided persona represent his experience of the outer world refracted through the distorting medium of his fantasies. As the action of the play progresses, the connections between Willy's inner world and external reality, which are tenuous enough to begin with, grow increasingly unstable and volatile. He is driven to kill himself, the ultimate act of self-deception in his struggle to impose his fantasies upon a reality that consistently thwarts his ambitions and will.[4]

The shifts in Willy Loman's mind between his dreams and actuality, on the level of his personal existence, and between fantasy and realism on the level of dramatic presentation, are conveyed in structural terms by the patterns in which the play's formal elements unfold to establish its dramatic rhythm. In the following analysis of Miller's play, we will take our cue from the conceptions of dramatic rhythm as set out by Paul M. Levitt and Kathleen George.[5] This analysis will show how much the rhythm of the play reinforces the "doubled" father/son and brother/brother relationships within it.

Not only is Willy Loman the chief character but it is primarily from his inner perspective that the play's dramatic action derives its meaning. The actual events enacted in his presence, particularly the return of his son Biff, become the trigger for Willy's recollections and fantasies which constitute the play's imaginary sequences. The significance of each of the play's episodes, as well as the structure of the plot as a whole, depends on the rhythmic alternations between actuality and Willy's mental responses to them. His ideal self-image and the reality of his actual behaviour and circumstances are the poles of both his inner existence and his dramatic interactions with the other characters. The personalities of each of the *dramatis personae* are connected specifically with a particular feature of Willy's inner self, with a particular stance he has adopted towards his environment, or with one of the values to which he has educated his sons. The conduct of the play's other characters is in great measure both the effect of his illusory perception of external reality and the cause of his deepening submersion into the world of his fantasies. When reality becomes too painful, Willy retreats into a dream world, consisting of his roseate recollections of the past and of fantasies in which he fulfils the aspirations, the attainment of which has eluded him in life.[6] Although his memories are based on actual events, these are falsified in his mind by wishful thinking about how they ought to have turned out. Hence in Willy's mind, reality as it is immediately experienced by him merges in his consciousness with his recollection of distant events to form a seamless continuum of past and present time.

Willy is torn between his need, on the one hand, to give expression to his innermost longings by establishing a direct and harmonious connection with nature and by manual labour; on the other, he wishes to maintain his place in society by creating a facade of emulous and combative self-assertiveness, which he tries to reconcile with his obsessive and desperate need to be admired and loved by others.[7] Together these contrary tendencies account for the conflicts both in his ideal conception of himself and in the way he conceives of others, in relation to the idealized image of his own personality. Moreover, Willy's ideal self-image is as fragmented as his real personality. Rather than consisting of a single coherent self, it is compacted of a number of contradictory selves, each of which might alone have formed the core of an integrated personality relatively free of tension, but which together make up an unstable persona that ultimately costs the protagonist his life.

Willy Loman spends much of his time on stage in an ongoing inner dialogue with a number of characters. Some, like Willy's son and his friend Charley, belong to the immediate and concrete reality which is being dramatized. The other figures emerge from Willy's recollections of the past and animate his inner world: his father, his older brother Ben, and old Dave Singleman. All three figures owe their presentation and description in the play to Willy's imagination, whose creation they essentially are. The characters that live through Willy's imagination are both the fruit and inspiration of this inner existence; and, by virtue of Willy Loman's function as the protagonist from whose perspective much of the play's action is seen, these characters furnish the focus of the clash of fantasy and reality in both Willy himself and the other *dramatis personae* of the play.

In Willy's consciousness each of the three men from the past has assumed the status of a personal hero and exemplar whom he aspires to emulate. Together they may constitute the end of the continuum between the ideal and the actual along which Willy's fluctuations between fantasy and reality take place. Each in his own right also furnishes Willy with a separate "ego ideal" that occupies a distinct place on a descending scale of proximity to the real world.[8]

Connected with Willy's past is the memory of his own father, who never assumes substantial form in Willy's mind but nonetheless powerfully informs his fantasy, primarily through his imagined conversations with Ben. Willy's father, the least accessible and most dimly remembered of the protagonist's exemplars, functions as his "absolute" ego ideal. His brother, Ben, against whose adventurous life and grand mercantile enterprises in far-off places Willy measures his own inadequacy and petty destiny, is his "desiderative" ego ideal. And last, Dave Singleman, the quintessence of the successful salesman and Willy's inspiration and model for feasible achievement, serves as the protagonist's "attainable" ego ideal.

Of these three ideal figures, Willy's father is the most remote from actuality and belongs to the very earliest and vaguest childhood recollections. Though not one of the *dramatis personae,* and only spoken of twice in the course of the play — during Ben's first "visitation" in Act One (pp. 156-57), and then briefly, by Willy, in Howard's office in Act Two (p. 180), his spirit dogs Willy and is repeatedly referred to on an auditory level by the sound of flute music. This is first heard as a sort of signature tune when the curtain goes up on the play, and is last heard when the curtain falls on the "Requiem". Hearing his father play the flute is about the only sensory memory Willy has of him — that and his father's "big beard". What we know of the picture in Willy's mind of the man, we learn from the description he receives from Ben's apparition. And what emerges from Ben's account is a part-mythical, part-allegorical figure. The image of him drawn by Ben is an emblematic composite of the classic types that are representative of America's heroic age: Willy's father is at once the untamed natural man and the westward-bound pioneer, the artisan, the great inventor, and the successful entrepreneur.

Willy's brother Ben represents an ideal which is closer to reality, that of worldly success, though on a scale so exalted as to be utterly beyond Willy's reach. To Willy's mind, Ben is the personification of the great American virtues of self-reliance and initiative by which an enterprising man may attain untold wealth; and it is through Ben that Willy tries to maintain personal connection with the myth of the individual's triumphant march from rags to riches.

In Willy's consciousness, Ben mediates between the domains of the ideal and the real. The aura of legend is nearly as strong in his brother as it is in his father. He, too, is a journeyer and adventurer. But what animates him in his travels appears to be less a hankering for the open road and the "grand outdoors" than the idea of the fortune to be made there. Sentiment plays no part in the tough maxims he tosses out to account for his success. Nor does he let family feeling cloud his purpose or divert him from his quest for riches, as is evident from the ease with which he abandons his search for his father to pursue diamond wealth in Africa or in the offhand manner in which he receives news of his mother's death. Even Willy gets short shrift from his older brother. Nevertheless, it is Ben's qualities of toughness, unscrupulousness, and implacability in the pursuit of gain that Willy wishes for himself and wants his boys to acquire.

Of Willy Loman's three personal heroes, Dave Singleman stands in the most immediate relation to the actuality of Willy's life. Neither the ideal of natural manhood personified by Willy's father nor the incarnation of freebooting enterprise embodied by his brother, Singleman represents success that is attainable. In Singleman the concept of success is cut down to Willy's size, reduced to an idea more nearly within his scope, that of getting ahead by being "well liked". Success as exemplified by Dave Singleman serves, as well, to sustain in Willy the feeling that though lacking in the daring and toughness that his father passed on to Ben, he too possesses an essential prerequisite for material achievement, one that he can bequeath to his own sons. So, poised in Howard's office between the phantoms of his dead brother and of Biff in his teens, Willy proclaims in an excess of confidence: "It's who you know and the smile on your face! It's contacts, Ben, contacts!" (p. 184).

Willy is not content merely to admire these men. He also internalizes their qualities and the ideas they represent, diminished and trivialising them in the process. The ideas of being in close touch with nature and taking to the open road that are inspired by Willy's memory of his father are reduced in his own life to puttering about in the back yard of his suburban Brooklyn home and making his routine rounds as a travelling salesman; the idea of venturesome private enterprise for high stakes represented by his brother depreciates to drumming merchandise for a commission; and even the example of Singleman's being "remembered and loved and helped by so many different people" (p. 180), over which Willy rhapsodises to Howard Wagner, is degraded in his own aspirations to the condition of being merely popular and well-liked.

Three of the characters among the principal *dramatis personae* of the play, Biff, Happy, and Charley, function in the real world as analogous to the ideal types in Willy's consciousness. Although none of them is a complete substantiation of Willy's ego ideals, each character has a dominant trait that identifies him with either Willy's father, or Ben, or Dave Singleman, and which determines Willy's relationship with him.

Biff, the returning son, most closely resembles his grandfather in rejecting the constraints imposed by the middle-class routines of holding down a job and making a living, and in his preference for the life of a drifter out West, working as a hired farmhand outdoors. He has a strong touch of the artist and dreamer in his temperament. He is also the most complex character of the three, the most at odds with himself. In this he closely resembles Willy. Like his father, Biff is torn between rural nostalgia and his need for solid achievement, and is tormented by the knowledge of personal failure. "I've always made a point of not wasting my life", he tells Happy, and then confesses to him, "and everytime I come back here I know that all I've done is to waste my life" (p. 139).

Happy corresponds to Ben, if only in a meagre and debased way. He shares his uncle's unscrupulousness and amorality, but has little of his singleness of purpose; and what he has of the last he dedicates to cuckolding his superiors at work and to the pursuit of women in general, activities that make up the only field in which he excels, as Linda recognizes when she sums him up as a "philandering bum" (p. 163). He also resembles Ben in the shallowness of his filial emotions. The trite praise he bestows on Linda - "What a woman! They broke the mold when they made her" (p. 169) - is on its own vulgar level as perfunctory and unfeeling as Ben's more elegantly phrased endorsement, "Fine specimen of a lady, Mother" (p. 155). However, some of his traits remind us of Willy, such as his bluster and nursing of injured pride, his insecurity about making good, as well as his philandering.

Charley is Dave Singleman brought down to earth. He has none of Singleman's flamboyance. Rather, his is a successful salesmanship domesticated. Singleman worked out of a hotel room. Charley maintains an office with a secretary and an accountant. He is stolid but honest and decent, and though not loved like Singleman, he is respected. And, by Willy's own startled admission towards the end, he is Willy Loman's only friend. He is also Willy's perfect foil, a man at peace with what he is and his place in the world.[9]

Except for Charley, the principal characters of *Death of a Salesman* share the same condition of being torn between the conflicting claims of ideality and actuality; and in this capacity the interrelations between them serve to extend and reinforce the rhythmic articulation of the play on a variety of formal levels. Among the consequences of the inner conflicts and contradictions of Willy Loman and his sons are their uncertainty and confusion concerning their own identities, admitted by each at some point in the play. Biff reveals to his mother, "I just can't take hold, Mom. I can't take hold of some kind of a life" (p. 161); Happy tells Biff, "I don't know what the hell I'm workin' for.. And still, goddamit, I'm lonely" (p. 139); and Willy confesses to Ben, "I still feel — kind of temporary about myself" (p. 159).[10]

Willy Loman's attitude to the real characters of the play is determined by their relation to the corresponding ideal types in his mind. None of the real characters is an unalloyed embodiment of these exemplars, who have all been debased to varying degrees in their corporeal counterparts. For example, Willy's most complex and ambivalent relationship is with Biff, who is associated most closely with Willy's absolute ego ideal.[11] It is of his older, "prodigal" son that Willy had always expected the most, and it is Biff's failure to live up to his expectations that grieves him the most. By comparison, his relationship with Happy, of whom he expects much less, is straightforward and indifferent. Willy's relationship with Charley is also determined by Charley's proximity to the ideal and his own distance from it. Because Charley comes the closest of everyone Willy knows to the attainable ideal he has set himself but failed to achieve, he treats him with a mixture of respect and envy. This is what prevents Willy from accepting Charley's offer of a job, because doing so would be tantamount to an admission of failure, a reason never stated explicitly by Willy but which Charley recognizes, as we learn during Willy's visit to Charley's office in the second act (p. 192):

> Charley: What're you, jealous of me?
> Willy: I can't work for you, that's all, don't ask me why.
> Charley: (Angered, takes out more bills) You been jealous of me all your life,
>   you damned fool! Here, pay your insurance.

By taking money from Charley instead, in the guise of a loan, Willy is able both to retain his self-esteem and to cling to his self-delusions. In a rare moment of candour, Willy privately acknowledges Charley's virtues and superiority to himself: "a man of few words, and they respect him" (p. 149); but for the most part he seeks to establish his own pre-eminence by belittling and hectoring him in petty ways, reminding Charley of his ignorance and inadequacy in ordinary matters: domestic repairs, diet, clothing, sports, cards, and so on.

To sum up, therefore, the function of all the principal characters in the play (apart from Linda) is determined by the operation of Willy's consciousness, suspended between reality and dreams. The measure of their moral significance to Willy is contingent on how far they have taken root in the ideal realm of his consciousness; and the extent to which they have done so is in inverse proportion to their actual presence in the dramatic sequences that take place in current time and space. Willy's father, the absolute ideal figure of the play, assumes the status of a recognizable personality only through the account of him received from the shade of his deceased brother in a scene that unfolds entirely in the mind of the protagonist. Otherwise, he is mentioned only once in the real action of the play, when Willy offhandedly refers to him as a prelude to his pathetic boast to Howard, "We've got quite a streak of self-reliance in our family" (p. 180). Ben's name too is hardly mentioned, and then only in passing, in the real dialogue of the play, and it is only in the fantasising episodes that he assumes palpable shape as a character. And finally Dave

Singleman, who serves Willy as a tangible, if illusory, example of success potentially within his grasp, comes alive in a present dramatic sequence of the play, even if only through the agency of words rather than personification. Significantly, the short eulogy to him that Willy delivers, and through which Singleman assumes dramatic life, comes at the moment when Willy is about to be fired and thereby deprived of the last vestige of hope for the attainable success Singleman represented.

The rhythm of the sequence of the two episodes focusing on sexual relations (the Boston woman and the restaurant scene where the boys pick up two women) is also a formal means serving a thematic idea.[12] The significance of the "Boston woman" is foreshadowed in Act One but also receives full dramatic revelation in the "restaurant scene" in Act Two, when it is reconstructed orally and visually so as to show its significance in the wider context of Willy's and Biff's relationship and their recognition of what is true and what is false in their lives.[13]   Whereas in the Boston scene it is the son who fails in social competition by flunking his test in mathematics, in the restaurant scene both father and son appear equally defeated in the economic and social struggle; and while in the Boston episode Biff, appalled by Willy's infidelity, realizes that his talkative, pretentious father is ineffectual (p. 207) and calls him a "phony little fake" (p. 208), in the restaurant scene Biff confesses to his father the pretensions and illusions of his own life too.   Happy's aggressive promiscuity is one other aspect of his latent "jungle" lifestyle.   He recognizes that his repeated, almost compulsive affairs with women related to higher executives at his work are an aspect of his "overdeveloped sense of competition" (p. 141). Thus, sexual infidelity is related to the tension between father and son and to the relationship between brother and brother.

The dramatic rhythm of *Death of a Salesman,* as manifested in the development of character, takes place through a complex interplay on the function of *dramatis personae* and their interplay with the three levels of Willy's consciousness: first, on the level of ideality; second on the level of fantasies and dreams; and last, on the level of his perception of concrete reality. It is from these three levels of consciousness that the protagonist's three ego ideals, the absolute, the desiderative, and the attainable, emerge.

Taken as a whole, Willy's three levels of consciousness dramatize his attitude to himself, to the others and to social reality.

A number of verbal references, which are also translated into stage effects, have symbolic significance and recur throughout the text of Miller's play. These echo and enhance the play's rhythmic design. Their significance derives from the associations they arouse in the protagonist's consciousness, where they are resolved into two principal symbolic clusters, connected with divergent attitudes that dominate Willy's imaginative life. It is interesting that these can be assigned to "father" and "brother" headings. The first cluster is connected with Willy's deep attachment to nature and his nostalgia for the countryside, feelings whose point of origin can be traced to Willy's father. The major references included in this cluster are to trees, seeds, and "travel" in its broadest sense. The second cluster is associated with commerce and enterprise of the kind personified for Willy by his brother Ben. The chief symbolic references of this cluster are to "jungle", Ben's watch and diamonds.

An evident pattern emerges in the way how the references to trees, wood, branches and leaves bind the domains of fantasy and reality in the play. They are clearly relevant to the ideal figure of Willy's father (a maker of flutes, a musical instrument of wood whose pastoral associations are immediate and altogether obvious), and to Willy's brother Ben (in whose vast tracts of Alaskan timberland Willy almost had a share).

Trees and leaves are the dominant stage effect when Willy's mind turns inward and towards the past, a time when his longings for a rural existence were more nearly satisfied. As he casts his mind back to a time when his home stood in what was still a landscape setting, the large elm trees that had once grown on his property form an important part of his recollections. In the dramatic present, the elms are gone and all that remains of the rural Brooklyn he had known is his backyard, which by the play's end is the setting of Willy's last effort to reassert control over events by planting vegetables in futile defiance of urban encroachment. For Willy, being truly happy means working with tools — "all I'd need would be a little lumber and some peace of mind" (p. 151), he says, hoping for a

better future. Trees are involved in his fantasies of Ben's success in the
jungle and in the "timberland in Alaska" (p. 183). Trees colour the
imagery of Willy's expressions of his inner desperation and need for help,
"the woods are burning" (pp. 152, 199). Trees and leaves are thereby
involved rhythmically in the linguistic constructs of the play as well as in
the visual setting of the stage: the memory of a hammock between the "big
trees" (p. 143), of seeds in the garden, of working on the wood ceiling, and
the lighting effect of the stage being "covered with leaves" (pp. 142, 151,
200). On the textual level, as well as on the stage, they become signs in the
theatrical system indicating the rhythm between fantasy and reality.

Willy's enthusiasm for the outdoors and the countryside is also
connected in his mind with the idea of travel and journeying. The idea of
travel is inseparable from the images he has of the ideal figures from his
past: his father driving his wagon and team of horses across the Western
states; Ben globetrotting between continents; and Dave Singleman
travelling in the smoker of the New York, New Haven and Hartford line.
His own life, too, is inseparable from travel, and the maintenance of the
family car is one of his major concerns. His car is essential to him for his
livelihood, and it is also the instrument by which he chooses to bring an
end to his life. It is the first thematically significant object to appear in the
dramatic text of the play, when it is mentioned in a context that
foreshadows the manner of Willy's death (p. 132).

The reference to nature is carried over to the second cluster of images
bearing on the theme of commerce and enterprise, but now appears in the
menacing guise of the "jungle", poles apart from the idyllic associations
aroused by the cluster of rural symbols. Its explicit connection with the
theme of enterprise and commerce, as well as its association with the
attendant idea of aggressive and unscrupulous competition, is fully
developed in the presence of all the principal characters in the scene of
Ben's first apparition (pp. 154-60). The specific verbal context in which the
reference first occurs is twice repeated almost verbatim by Ben: "... when
I was seventeen I walked in to the jungle, and when I was twenty-one I
walked out. And by God I was rich" (pp. 157, 159-160). On the first
occasion when Ben speaks these words he does so at Willy's urging for the

benefit of the boys. The second time, is on his departure and they are uttered for Willy's ears alone. What happens between the two utterances brings out the thematic significance of the passage as referring to the rule of the jungle that governs the sort of enterprise that Ben represents. And the event that drives this particular moral home is the sparring match between Ben and Biff, in which Ben departs from the rule of fair play and declaims the precept, "Never fight fair with a stranger, boy. You'll never get out of the jungle that way" (p. 158). By the time Ben's shade departs, Willy seems to have taken Ben's point when he chimes in with great enthusiasm, "That's just the spirit I want to imbue them with! To walk into the jungle! I was right!" (p. 160). But the truth is that Willy was wrong. Ben's lesson is not about going into jungles, but coming out of them, alive and prosperous. The watch and diamond references are associated through Ben with the "jungle" reference. Their connection with one another, and their symbolic bearing on commerce, become obvious once their association with the ideas of time and wealth are established, and we recall that these are proverbially equated in the businessman's adage that time is money.

The watch and diamond references are also merged by a specific object in the play: the "watch fob with a diamond in it" that Ben had given to Willy, and Willy had it pawned to finance Biff's radio correspondence course (p. 160). Thus, time and money, the two cherished commodities of business, are turned in Loman's hands to loss rather than profit.

Willy, as a son, is inwardly completely dependent on the idol of a father he has created, compared to whom all other imagined, idealized figures can only be a reduction. He relates to his own sons according to his own wishful, ideal self-images. On this scale Biff, the returning son, is the focus of Willy's outer aspirations as well as his disappointments. Willy ends his life realising that Biff does love him, but mistakenly rewarding him with "outer" benefits — the life insurance. Biff by now understands his dead father and forgives him his misjudged life. The "sin" here is of a father who could not adjust his inner self to an outward, changing reality. The father, paradoxically, is forgiven by the son, who gains a better understanding of himself.

It is the sin-guilt-innocence aspect of the archi-pattern which is prominent in *Death of a Salesman*. This aspect is transferred to the father figure, Willy, whose frustration over his failure has become part and parcel of the characters and the lives of his failing sons. Both father and sons are "lost". But while the father chooses death as the only way out, the sons, at the end of the play, turn outwards to engage with life in different terms: Happy as "Number One" in the jungle, and Biff as a man who has gained a deeper understanding of his father and of himself.

Biff's real return home is when he is freed from the web of falsehood created by his father's value judgements. His search for identity culminates when he achieves humility through self-knowledge. His return is an extension of Willy's tragic search for himself and for his father in others, as son, brother and father.

BIRTH, RETURN AND DEATH IN THE WOMB OF LANGUAGE
WHO'S AFRAID OF VIRGINIA WOOLF?

"...our son is...dead".

This play represents an essential change from those considered so far. In *Who's Afraid of Virginia Woolf?* the "inward" return is to inwardness itself. In other words, the setting for this play is not the home but the soul, in fact, the souls of the parents. Plot segments of the archi-pattern appear in a muted, displaced form: the "secret" is there, but connected to an invented character, the son; the "wandering" and "recognition" segments may be seen as an internal cathartic process in the part of the parents, not the son.[1] The thematic aspects, likewise, appear in an introverted form, as echoes of inner needs, metaphorically substituted in language.

The son does not exist because no womb bore him, but he is formed and birthed by the womb of language: "Oh, Martha; no, you labored...how you labored" (George, p. 217). It is only the growing consciousness that the creation of the son by language fulfils a deep need on the. part of his parents which eases his birth: "It was an easy birth...once it had been...accepted, relaxed into" (Martha, p. 217). It is by language, too, that he is ultimately put to death.

Martha's yearning to be an "earth mother" and her struggle against her actual barrenness, are expressed and compensated by a metaphoric-linguistic web within which she gives birth to her son: "He was a healthy child, a red, bawling child, with slippery, firm limbs..". (Martha, p. 218). George aids and coaches her in weaving this linguistic web around the son. He effectively plays midwife, but he also takes upon himself the responsibility of killing the son by means of language. The right to kill the son "in sorrow", as he was born "in sorrow" is his, so: "I have the right, Martha. We never spoke of it; that's all. I could kill him any time I wanted to" (p. 236).

Between layers of language, between silence and playful outbursts, the son lives, dies and is lost. The play consists of a succession of "play-games" within which life and death are subject to the rule of language. This process lies at the heart of the dramatic strategy of *Who's Afraid of Virginia Woolf.* Language here exists as a prediscursive reality, in which George and Martha's characters are moulded, and in which the son is born. He is an expression of the dire state of their internal world, as well as a way of reviving and sustaining some means of communication between them.[2]

The theories of Lacan on the divide between the imaginary and the symbolic, taken in their simplest form, provide a useful tool for analysing the "language" of this play, which, as stated, is central to it. Some of Lacan's basic terms might provide signposts for a discussion of this play, and a short summary of these follows.[3]

Lacan's starting point is the theories of psychoanalysis; he applies their principles to the theory of language. He links the idea of Freud's unconscious interaction between the ego and the id to the structure of relationships between parents and children as they are constituted in language. Humans enter a pre-existent system of signifiers which take on meaning within a language system. Lacan postulates that men, women and children are only linguistic signifiers of an inner "desire" which cannot be expressed because discourse is based on conventions, prohibitions and inhibitions. These linguistic signifiers form a register which covers up the friction of the primary system of relationships within the family.

According to Lacan, the relationship between infant and mother is one of "specular image" (i.e., mirror image). The mother is the "I-Ideal" for the infant. But at 18 months, when the infant enters language, a trio is created: the father joins the infant and mother. The infant then recreates the I-Ideal relationship with the parent of the same sex, but this time, with the entrance of language, the relationship contains conventions and prohibitions.[4] The relationship with the father is triple: with the organic creator (the real father), the father of the I-Ideal (the imaginary father) and the father who is masked with names and metaphors (the symbolic father).[5] It is the symbolic realm which is most closely connected to that of language.

Language cannot formulate unconscious elements of desire. Pre-linguistic signifiers of the unconscious are a source of disruption to the symbolic order. Language never succeeds completely in covering the "hole" between the "needs" of the infant, which existed before language and continue to exist in the unconscious, and the "demand" for satisfaction which is expressed in language. The moulding of needs by discourse does not give any satisfaction, and leaves behind it a "desire". This desire is expressed in signifiers — dreams, jokes and art in all its manifestations.

Discourse analysis based on Freud and Lacan postulates that the unconscious is expressed in a rhetoric of signifiers which constitute a language whose rules are not expressed, or indeed known, consciously. Analysis of discourse, therefore, cannot be based solely on speech and language formations. It must also take into account the "deficit" expressed in its semantic and pragmatic content.

Using these terms, which have obviously been considerably simplified and condensed, as our starting point, let us now turn to some central questions raised by the function of language in *Virginia Woolf*. Is it George's and Martha's "desire" which creates their son in the realm of language? What is the "demand", which the birth, return and death of the son in language, is supposed to answer? A textually-based analysis of the characterization of George and Martha reveals that their inner worlds, and also their imagined son, exist by virtue of a linguistic strategy which uses what is not expressed, what is hinted at and what is garbled to cover the "holes" within them.[6]

One particular episode, called here the "bergin/bourbon" episode, may be used as a kind of paradigm of the linguistic revelation/concealment which is typical of the play as a whole. It is retold three times by George and Martha. First, George tells it as the story of an outing to a gin-mill with his friends. One of the friends "had killed his mother with a shotgun some years before — accidentally, completely, without even an unconscious motivation" (p. 94). This friend drank a lot (forbidden during Prohibition) and when his turn came to order, wanting bourbon, asked for "bergin, give me some bergin, please...bergin and water" (p. 95). This lapse amused the whole "dive", and got him and his friends a free round of drinks from "the management, by the gangster-father of one of us". George goes on to recount how this friend's father was killed in a road accident: the youth himself, who was driving had swerved to avoid a porcupine.

The second time the episode emerges is when Martha reminds George, "You used to drink bergin too" (p. 123). She tells him this apparently in private, but it is aimed at Nick, too. After this she tells her own version of the story of the 15-year old who killed his parents, and who later used the episode as the pivot of the plot of a book he wrote (pp. 136-7). The third time the episode appears is when George describes his own "son's" death in a road accident, whose details strongly resemble those of the accident in the first episode (p. 231).

How can these three versions of the same "bergin/bourbon" episode serve as a key to the dramatic strategy of the play? They can be used as epitomisers of the way that language reveals what it conceals. The truth of "bourbon" is diverted and only hinted at by "bergin", the garbled version. Three important elements of George's version are foregrounded in the other versions: the Janus figure of the father and the son (George as father and as son, the father/son accident, the gangster-father's offer of drinks); separation between the private and public realm of language (the inner life of the youth as opposed to the public sphere of the gin mill);

and most important, the dubious actuality of the events, the difference between empirical truth and imagined truth.

The Janus figure of the father and the son appears in all three of the versions. In the first, the son who has killed the father in a road accident, and an additional father-figure, the "gangster", also appears. In the second, Martha's father forbids George to publish his book, which Martha claims is an autobiography. In the final version, the son who kills his father becomes the father who kills his son.[7]

George unsuccessfully suppresses "bourbon", as is hinted at by the presence of "Prohibition" and "gangsters". The hint in public of the thing suppressed is, as George later phrases it, the washing of "dirty underthings in public". The banality and vulgarity of the hint pollutes the search for the understanding of others and the struggle for a private, intimate way of expression. The space between the private and intimate and the public and normative is inhabited by the "laugh", which serves as a form of expression for the "deficit" which exists there. The laughter of the dive trails the "bergin/bourbon" youth and pursues him to the asylum, where it becomes his only form of expression. It is society's scorn (and indeed his own) of his inability to mould himself in language, of his having to resort to garbled speech. The laugh appears again in another episode set between the private and the public. George reacts sarcastically to Martha's disappointment over his status and his appearance at social university gatherings by saying "Martha didn't think I laughed loud enough" (p. 25).

The third element of the "bergin/bourbon" story is "Truth and illusion. Who knows the difference, eh, toots? Eh?" (p. 201). This explicit statement appears a number of times and expresses the character of the play as a whole, suspended between the referential and the metaphoric register. The facts in common in the three versions link them to the referential register, but the differences and occasional contradictions among them reveal the "deficit" in their metaphoric nature.[8]

In the final stage of the play, the process of linguistic reincarnation which makes the "bergin" take precedence over the "bourbon" reaches its climax. Martha and George know that their wars of language expressing their "demand" cannot cover their inexpressible pain.

The abysmal pain which exists within the two main characters cannot be solved by the intrasubjective function of language, neither can it find any cure on the intersubjective level. In the rounds of their linguistic games, each feels abandoned and alone, but they cling to each other with continuous outbursts of verbal competition, through which they both try to find a cure for their own despair while attempting to answer the "needs" of the other. In these games, a self-contained reality exists, in which consciousness of the gap between emotional life and the possibility of creating linguistic discourse is occasionally expressed. In playing out the "bits" they almost forego the chance of communication via language. They retreat from the reflective dimension, and only use language to evoke themselves and each other, attempting to express their "needs".[9] George and Martha also try to find a way of satisfying their fathers' "needs", and conclude this protracted process by the birth and death of their son by means of language.

George, in his role as son, has aspired all his life to satisfy his father's "needs". The "bergin" hints at the inner self he cannot express. George's father is a kind of "signifier" for him: all his life he pursues him, searching for him. George's chain of signifiers, loaded with different icons of fatherhood and additional constellations of father/son relationships, create a "symbolic order". Each stage of his search for his father ends with the father's being lost and George's failure to identify with him. This failure in father/son relationships is tied intimately to language. The first father is the "real", physical father, whom George "kills" in the road accident. The father icon changes to an "imaginary father", the authoritative character who embodies normative rules and prohibitions. George wants to satisfy this father's "needs" by offering him his linguistic creation (the story of the killing of the father). But this offering is not accepted. George reaches the third stage of the symbolic order, the "symbolic father". At this stage, he shifts the father image onto himself, and creates a son in language, with the help of a mother/woman. But, the metaphorical and textual games played around the constellation of father/mother/son cannot satisfy the "need" of George as a son. Underneath the language, a "hole" is exposed, which cannot be covered by games, whether played by George or by Martha. The creation turns on his creator, as George says to Martha, "you've started playing variations on your own distortions" (p. 155). The language which gave birth to the son becomes a "club" in their arguments, and beats them into the territory of madness. The love-hate, attraction-repulsion which George and Martha have for each other disintegrates into mutual recriminations, and also leads to the killing of the son returning home. This "killing" might open the possibility of a new life, beyond language.[10]

Martha admires her father and her life's ambition has been to satisfy his "needs".[11] George's opinion that her father has effectively deserted her and has no interest in her fate only serves to accentuate her submission to her father's will, and the depth of her sense of frustration and failure when she does not succeed in fulfilling his expectations. "I more or less grew up with him. Jesus, I admired that guy!...I worshiped him...(p. 77). Her father knows "how to run things" (p. 27), and as President of the university, an authoritative and task-oriented man, would have wished to pass his powers down to his son: "Daddy has a sense of history, of continuation" (p. 79). But since the desired son is a daughter, who cannot fulfil this role within accepted norms, she is driven to seek a male substitute for herself.[12] The search for the son/bridegroom who is to take her place splits into two figures based on her father's ideals: body and brain. "Daddy says a man is only partly brain...he has a body, too, and it's his responsibility to keep both of them up...you know?" (p. 55). Her first marriage satisfied the "body" dimension. The young gardener she chose "mowed the lawn at Miss Muff's, sitting up there, all naked, on a big mower, mowing away" (p. 78). Her father annulled this marriage and Martha was left "on the look out" (p. 79) for the "brain". "And along he came, bright eyed, into the — History Department" (p. 81). Martha stresses that her marriage to George as a son/bridegroom was her idea, not her father's. When George disappointed her father's expectations, and therefore hers, and could not or would not be "groomed", a "son" was born who could satisfy all her father's wishes. Initially, she even claims that his eyes, like her father's, are green, not brown like hers or blue like George's. It is only at the end of the play that George gives the son eyes which contain elements of all three, "blue, green, brown" (p. 220), and Martha gives her silent consent to this.

The realm of "bergin", which emerges instead of the expected "bourbon", is also expressed in the justification for killing the son. The reason given for the killing is that Martha "broke the rules of the game". George claims that Martha "brought it out into the open" (70). Her attack on the divide between the private, intimate sphere of linguistic creation and its public exposure is what requires that the chapter be brought to an end. However, Martha's revelation of the existence of the son to Honey occurs within the first third of the play, but the son is not killed until the end, when "total war" has been declared. This delay requires an explanation. It points to the fact that George's affective responses do not spring from the revelation of the "secret" of the son, but instead from his own growing frustration and disappointment in his own internal father/son conflict and in the father/male he is for Martha.[13] The "secret" is, therefore, assigned by the "bergin". George's outbursts of anger and pain throughout the three scenes are not tied to the image of the son, but to himself as a son.

In the first act, there is an episode dealing with boxing, which is told by Martha. Martha's father challenged George to a boxing match: "come on, young man...what sort of son-in-law are you?" (p. 56), and George was reluctant to accept the challenge. As a result Martha put on the gloves, admitting "I didn't know why I did it", and knocked George to the floor: "And it was an accident...a real, goddam accident!" (p. 57). She fears that this episode "colored our whole life". In fact, it is a non-verbal model for their joint inability to satisfy the father, an outlet into the pre-linguistic.

The existence of the imaginary son, his birth and his return/death, are only an echo of a deeper structure in which Martha and George struggle with the search for a father. This is particularly evident in the passages in which George is the subject of conflict, which lead to the most violent of his outbursts. Three times George is driven to physical violence, each a result of his being personally hurt. The first occasion directly follows the story of the boxing, in which he was humiliated by Martha in front of her father; it ends in his trying to kill Martha with the Chinese parasol. The second follows the "perfect match" episode, when Martha calls him "a great...big...fat...flop! George is moved to tears and threats with a broken bottle (pp. 84-85). The third outburst is in the second act, "Walpurgisnacht", after Martha gives her version of the story of the youth, and tells that George was the youth who confessed to her father, "No sir, this isn't a novel at all...this is the truth...this really happened...to me! (p. 137). The three occasions when George is driven to physical rather than verbal violence, then, are all a direct result of George's being insulted and attacked himself, and have no overt connection with the revelation of the secret of the son.

In the second act of the play his physical outbursts, which were as a result of his being humiliated as a son or husband, diminish. Instead, George himself assumes the role of the father, and creates the ritual of the death of the son in language only, just as he previously used language to kill or assault father-figures.[14]

The son has by now has reached the age of twenty one — adulthood — in their imaginations. Despite this, however, he is not able to satisfy the "needs" of his "parents", the "hole" they have. He has become only another object by which they measure their failure. The evocation of the son's return, and then of his death, is a necessary linguistic-imaginative act.[15] His death makes George's and Martha's "desire" an eternal fact of life, an internal "hole" of pain which both must learn to live with.

Nick and Honey, as many scholars have claimed, are analogous to George and Martha. The men share academic careers; the women's development is restricted, and they both revere a father/God. Both couples have a child which neither woman has been able to bear, but whose existence is an affective focus for them. Nick and Honey form a kind of shadow which emphasises the main characters, but which is devoid of the linguistic dimension that highlights the gap between what is revealed and what is concealed.

In Nick's story two elements are stressed: Honey's father and her phantom pregnancy, which are analogous, as we have said, to George and Martha's own story. This analogy exists not just in the father/daughter relationship and the "death" of a child, but also in the revelation of a private story in public. Honey blames Nick: "You told them!" (p. 147), and Nick answers, "Honey, I didn't mean to..". This is a reversal of the situation between George and Martha.

The areas in which George fails, and which provide Martha with material to embarrass him in public, are the same areas which Honey mentions as a source of pride in her relationship with Nick. According to Honey, Nick was a footballer (p. 51), but he "...was much more... adept at boxing, really" - contrast George's failure in the area of "body". Nick, who took his Masters when he was exceptionally young, stands also in opposition to George's slow academic progress in the area of "mind".

Nick has no "bergin/bourbon" aspect, though he echoes this by "I'll stick to bourbon, I guess" (p. 30). He embodies all that George will not or cannot be: ambitious, task-oriented and conformist. Nick at once arouses George's contempt and his apprehension.

It is interesting to note that there is also a suggestive father/son dimension in the relationship between Nick and George. George feels a certain degree of closeness to this young man who is the very embodiment of the hopes that Martha and her father vested in him. George, in his sarcastic way, tries to get closer to Nick and to warn him of the danger to his personal autonomy if he lets himself conform to the rat-race of academic life. Nick, who could almost be a son to George, does not respond to these fumbling advances, thus intensifying George's jealousy and pain, and ultimately his pity. George, consciously or subconsciously, and with seriousness mixed with sarcasm, ascribes his own and his "son's" characteristics to Nick: he constantly puts Nick in the History, not the Biology department, he repeats that Nick is twenty-one, despite Nick's statement that he is twenty-eight (p. 34). The climax of this process is when George greets Nick with "Sonny, you've come home for your birthday! At last!" (p. 195).

Who's Afraid Of Virginia Woolf? has social/historical and cultural/mythical aspects, which give an added dimension to the emotional gaps that exist within the characters and to the links among them. Mention of historical phenomena (Berlin, China, Western culture, genetic engineering) gives the play an anchor in time, but in skimming over these matters it emphasises the detachment and lack of involvement of the two protagonists, who live in their own world and play with each other. The names of the two protagonists recall George and Martha Washington, evoking the American myth of success. Achievement, materialism and the race for status are the heritage of all of the characters, be it in the realm of administration, preaching or academic advancement.[16]

Within the play, there are those who have reached or are attempting to reach the top of the ladder, those who wish to eternalise their status in their children, and those who are sick of the competition and regard themselves as a sad, but honourable, failure. The desire for success, therefore, exists in the realm of social and historical expectations which informs the American Dream, as well as in the personal realm.[17] The fact that George and Martha try to fulfil their fathers' expectations shows that they are chasing this myth, too, as an alternative to the present. Martha's seduction of Nick is not just an act of defiance of George, but also an attempt to find the fusion of brain and body which is the symbol of American success. The ambivalent relationship George has with Nick shows elements of the successful all-American boy myth.

Three areas of culture are to be found in the play, within the dialogue and within the characterization of the dramatic *personae*: biology (Nick and Honey), history (George) and art in its mythic and linguistic representations (George and Martha). Biology (which is sometimes substituted by mathematics) is sarcastically termed by George as the science of the future, which will create "a race of men test-tube bred, incubator-born...superb and sublime" (p. 65). Later, George points to Nick as an exemplar of this new race.

George is "preoccupied with history" (p. 50). He is directed by the past, which carries within it the germ of the future. George's attitude is also linked to his personal and family life. According to him, within personal and family history, the link with the future is missing: "People do...have kids. That's what I mean about history" (p. 40). The futuristic, biological view of the world lacks continuity with the past: "history will be eliminated" (p. 67). George's obsession with history covers his internal "hole" in both the collective and personal areas. Futurism offers him no continuity, and he has no personal continuity and no child either. This double subjective disappointment (conscious and subconscious) of his aspirations to cover the "hole" impels him to creativity in the linguistic area.

In this area he makes use of other authors but is himself the primary creator.[18] His linguistic myth of the son is set in a continuum between the real (biological/historical) and the metonymic (metaphoric). But here too he finds that he is unsatisfied, and is reaching the very limits of his ability. The only hope which remains is "something inside the bone...the marrow...and that's what you gotta get at" (p. 213).

The "marrow" which George and Martha "get at" at the end of their journey is linguistic abstinence. They recognize that social lies and a skin of linguistic games cannot ease the pain of the "hole" which eats into their souls. The only thing left is fear, and the faint possibility of returning to themselves beyond language, in silence.

The existence of silence as a possible place to come home to, beyond the links that language makes between people, is hinted at in another place in the text. In his "bergin/bourbon" story, George tells of the youth who was institutionalised for thirty years, during which he "has...not uttered one...sound" (p. 96). He admires the tranquillity of the institutionalised: "They [insane people] maintain a...a firm-skinned serenity...the...the under-use of everything leaves them...quite whole" (p. 97). Here there is a hint that George yearns for total silence, and that this yearning is what lurks behind his verbal pyrotechnics.

George's journey towards language, and then away from it, can be compared to the journey of the son in the archi-pattern. But here, a new stage has been reached: the son never returns home. George's own insistent yearning for death is evident in his son's death, something he connects with the son his spirit has created — "A son who is, deep in his gut, sorry to have been born" (p. 227) — who must, thereafter, die in a ritual of exorcism of false spirits.[19]

The process of linguistic signification constitutes a parallel process between unconscious and the conscious subjectivity. The expression which tries to cover the "hole" within George moves from the personal to the public, and from an oral story ("bergin/bourbon") to become a "memory book". At the end of the play, when George can no longer satisfy his own and Martha's needs with language, he apparently receives a written telegram, which he then eats. The process of reduction of the linguistic plane is also expressed in the continuum which exists between George and Martha's verbal creations, the "requiem" section (p. 227), where Albee stipulates that they speak over each other, and the end of the play (p. 239 ff.), by which time they have diminished into monosyllables. The play ends with "Silence".

How does the prodigal son archi-pattern appear, then, in this drama? The returning son is in fact the father here, who, as a son, is engaged in a continual search for his father.[20] This search moves from the "real" father, transmuted into an ideal father, to the metaphor of the son. This process exists entirely in language, which gives birth to sons as well as killing them. The womb of language creates the "real" father in writing, in the book which Martha calls George's "brainchild"; the birth/return/death of the son is created in speech. When both writing and speech are proved disappointments, and cannot fulfil George's and Martha's deepest needs, a stage of great silence is reached. The return of the son to his home is only, therefore, the possibility of return to oneself. The recognition is only "peeling of labels" from the ego, and from the illusion of understanding the other. Forgiveness is expressed in the few references to pity, often with Biblical overtones. The silence becomes more concentrated towards the end of the play, and at its centre is the hope that the father/son/daughter will return home, to himself/herself.

DECONSTRUCTION OF THE RETURN TO THE FAMILY
ROMANCE: *THE HOMECOMING*

"...but nevertheless, we do make up a unit".

In *The Homecoming* the stage set is the family parlour, the characters are members of a family, and the theme recalls Ibsen's treatment of generational conflict, marital relationships and a returning son.[1] The play operates in the tension between two dichotomic dimensions of reality: the empirical and comprehensible, and the irrational and not perceivable.[2] The juxtaposition of a conceivable empirical reality with an implausible one coincides with conflict between constituent behaviour modes and their violation; this directory evokes suspense, irony and pathos, and both moves and terrifies us.

The home and the homecoming are never ultimately defined. The returning son demonstrates an enigmatic presence as well as absence. The motivation for his return, his bearing and the circumstances of his departure are obscure and undermine our perception of homecoming while at the same time opening it to endless varieties of feasibility and moral judgment.[3] The schema used here to illuminate the expectation and reality of homecoming is based on two overlapping phases within the play: the constructive and the deconstructive.

This play will be analysed by concentrating on the nature of homecoming and how this is constructed and deconstructed. Ultimately this will lead us to the conclusion that the archi-pattern has effectively been reversed, and that the emphasis has moved from the prodigal to the family to which he returns.

These theoretical terms, which are from Structuralist and Deconstructuralist theory, are used in accordance with the various theorists whose methodology they avoid while still keeping them in general perspective. "Constructive" (and likewise "structure") refers here to a chain of dramatic signifiers organized as elements of a schema, supposed to signify a stable phenomenological and moral entity. "Deconstruction" here represents a system in which the signifier defies the orderly requirement of the signified by being open-ended and non-teleological.

In the frame of constructing realistic premises, the characters keep up a conventional facade of family life: they live together, although each character seems to be economically independent; they join and share interest in jobs and hobbies, memories and experiences; and they have rebuilt the house to contain a large family room. They keep a place for their missing son, who returns, hoping to find his former home and to be recognized by the family. All the characters demand a share in the family house. Max and Sam claim ownership of their parents' house, Lenny demonstrates his claim in occupying a room downstairs, and Teddy returns looking for the home he left. But, as A. E. Quigley phrased it, "the play deals not just with the nature of homes but with the nature of homecoming".[4] This would-be realistic encounter with family life is distorted and shattered by the constant effort of the family members to find their functional identities through a power struggle.[5] They create wishful images of themselves and wrestle for a dominant position in domestic and extra-domestic roles while exploiting each other for their needs. These mutual exploitations are expressed in terms of sexual possessiveness and aggressive conduct.[6]

The deconstructive strategy of this power struggle is achieved through theatrical and linguistic means that not only signify but also oblique.[7] These are evident in the lack of any guilt feelings towards other characters or towards a specific event. The characters speak about morality, but act otherwise and are indifferent to the breaking of codes by themselves or by others. The element of sin — of guilt and innocence — is missing in sexual as well as generational relationships and in the reworking of the archi-pattern of the prodigal son, who, as no defined sin exists, is a returning son.

The dramatic devices used to exploit the tensions between phases of homecoming are connected to a known element of Pinter's style: a plot which is not devised as a single constellation but more as a lasting condition. In this play, the overall presentation of the plot juxtaposes dramatic episodes: scenes from the past are recreated and distorted in the present, and sequences are connected verbally but their epistemological and moral premises are changed. The temporal reference indicates a collapse of sequential development as the plot is constantly and variously reshaped. The dialogue is not identical with the action on stage and not in proportion to the specific situation. It contains elements which are disharmonious with the overall intention, and it is interrupted by "pauses" and instructions for "silence" which carry internalized aggression.

The main strategy of *The Homecoming,* however, is based on a schema of memory-stories constructed of present and past family reality and the return of the son, expected to be conventional, which are deconstructed.

Memory and its refutation are central to many of the "micro-stories", (short narrative segments) in *The Homecoming,* as well as being a central motif in many of Pinter's other plays: *Landscape* (1968), *Silence* (1969), *Night* (1969) and *Old Times* (1971). The first three of these are mainly about exchanging recollections and living on in different worlds: in *Old Times,* the exchange of memories in a domestic situation is deconstructed in another, leaving the characters paradoxically together but alone. In *The Homecoming,* the function of memory-stories is even more articulated. The contradictions they create do not delve into the possibility of communication, but defy the image of family life and of coming home to it. The micro-stories in *The Homecoming* appear to give expression to the memories of the various characters, but the process of their deconstruction begins as soon as they are spoken, in their clash with the reality appearing on the stage. They are further deconstructed when various plot or character elements from them subsequently appear as fragments, inverted or condensed, in other contexts. In the stories there is a continuous process of breaking models of rational and normative behaviour. The fragments become part of new constellations, which are related to the past but are themselves flawed. A continuum of construction and deconstruction is created.[8]

Much of the construction and deconstruction process is evident in the dramatization of present and mainly past familial interrelationships. In the diachronic process of the drama a synchronic structure may be observed in which there is an interplay between the micro-stories as told by different characters and the dramatic situation. The micro-stories deal with what happened to a person, and are related as reminiscences by the *dramatis personae*. T.E. Postelwait claims that in this play "the matrix is one of time intersecting with space". The diachronic mode, expressed in a "language of memory", intersects with the synchronic mode conceived in spatial terms as a struggle for power in a family home.

All phases of deconstruction are ambiguous, as every deviation can be recognized only when measured by conventional standards, and neither of the constructive and deconstructive phases is intact as each contains elements of the other. The phase of narrative construction is juxtaposed with deconstructive elements of stage presentation; or the micro-stories themselves are expressed in phrases of aggressive encounter or elements of one micro-story are displaced — all these evidencing destructive elements.

The dramatic repetition of events, whole or partial, revolves around the uncreating of the past. The micro-stories about family life or about individual virility are taken to pieces and shattered. Doubt is cast on the credibility of memories by connected sequences which repeat an event or part of it, nullifying not only its probability but also the norms on which it is based. The event is contradicted either by the narrator himself or by another character, or is distorted by over-emphasis which strays from reality. For example, in Lenny's micro-story about a "certain lady" having "the pox", the following exchange occurs:

Ruth: How did you know she was diseased?
Lenny: How did I know? (Pause)
       I decided she was (p. 31).

Another example might be Max's memory of Jessie which he relates to Ruth:

Max: Trouble? What are you talking about? What trouble? Listen, I'll tell you
       something. Since poor Jessie died, eh, Sam? we haven't had a woman
       in the house. Not one. Inside this house. And I'll tell you why.
       Because their mother's image was so dear any other woman would
       have...tarnished it!   But you...Ruth...you're not only lovely and
       beautiful, but you're kin. You're kith. You belong here (p. 75).

There are ironic contradictions in this speech, mainly relating to the gap between the presentation of the memory of Jessie as a model figure and the inference we can draw from the play as a whole that she, too, may have been a prostitute. Ruth's behaviour with Joey and Lenny seems to be the reason for her being accepted: other women would have "tarnished" Jessie's blameless image. This is clearly ironic too.

Sometimes, as mentioned, the coherent attitude towards an event is over-emphasised and diverges from the accepted rituals of daily life — the exchange between Lenny and Ruth about the glass of water, for example, or the discussions about the cheese roll, or the importance the characters assign to sitting and standing. Some of the micro-stories also destabilise accepted norms through over-emphasising — Lenny's memory of the "old lady". In content and in style they contradict what is expected in human relations. A tension is created between words and situations. Memories seem to be faulty, and the present is constantly isolated from the past.

Many of the micro-stories, which are constructed around episodes of family romance and its deconstruction, work in three relationship areas: parent/child, sibling and gender. They serve as a battleground in which the teller attempts to assert himself by threatening the other characters' security, thus acquiring status and admiration. In his own stories, each teller constructs a reality of which he is the centre and which supports his physical, communicative and social strength as well as his sexual potency and/or his ability to awaken love. Power and sex are interrelated, as are the axes of the great majority of the micro-stories in the play, centered mainly on the convention episodes of "family love". These stories are deconstructed, and the process sheds light on relationships in general and homecoming to familial relationships in particular.

The first micro-story is told by Max. It concerns the power and virility of his friend MacGregor. Max ascribes this power and vitality to himself too, although the best Max can show now for such a vital past are his "scars".

> We were two of the worst hated men in the West End of London. I tell you,
> I still got the scars. We'd walk into a place, the whole room'd stand up, they'd
> make way to let us pass (p. 8).

The real importance of this speech is how it shows the invasion of Max's imagined past external life into his present home life, his own family context. He brings desires from one area into the other. He would like his family to stand up and make way when he walks in, too.

In this micro-story he also refers to his missed opportunity, because of "family obligations", for a career as a trainer, for which he "had a gift" (p.10). Part of this gift is the ability to tell a good filly (preferable to colts) by looking her in the eye. This sensual quality, combined with his aggressiveness, only hinted at here, is further developed in his other micro-stories. Doubt is cast, subsequently, on the epistemological truth and moral stability of Max's memories about his missed life opportunities.

The next micro-story by Max is composed of his memories of "our father" (p. 19); the important point here is the number of verbs in the speech, filling it with actions that hint at violence ("came", "looked down", "bent over", "pick up", "handle me", "wipe and pat me", "pass me", "toss me", "catch me"). The cuddled baby could be a colt, being aggressively tended by his trainer. Here, the style of the micro-story itself is part of the deconstruction process, with the vocabulary creating doubt about this ideal father/son tableau and about the family romance of "I remember my father" (p. 19).

The third "memory" of Max is about brothers, fathers and sons. It is constructed again on a conventional episode in family life — the legacy of the father. The construction phase, the father's words, "Max, look after your brothers" (p. 39), is immediately deconstructed: "How could he say that if he was dead?" (ibid.), and is followed by a verbal attack on Sam, full of impotence, blood and violence. The supposedly caring brotherly relations are further desconstructed towards the end of the play, Sam's passivity climaxes in an apparent death which is disregarded by Max. His only reaction to Sam's death is that the "corpse" might dirty the carpet.[9]

Another aspect of the ideal family which is evoked by Max is the bringing home of the bride. This is told not in a single micro-story but is referred to three times: when he sarcastically suggests that Sam bring home a wife (p. 15), when he accepts Ruth as his daughter-in-law (p. 49) and when he invites Teddy to bring home his next wife (p. 59). The triumphant bringing home of the bride is triply deconstructed by the context, respectively by the mention of Sam's homosexual inclinations, the suggestion that Ruth might be a prostitute, and the implication that Teddy should continue to support his family by introducing another wife-prostitute.

The most revealing micro-story is the memory of a family evening: Max, the working father, coming home, taking care of his three sons, cherishing his wife and enjoying a family reunion (p. 6). Here he evokes a past that climaxes in a tableau of the Madonna and children, a hyperbolic family ideal.[10] This micro-story is mainly deconstructed only at the very end of the play, when it is done most forcefully: Ruth sits on Max's chair, the patriarchal throne, and Max, Joey and Lenny arrange themselves around her. This final tableau of family life is a deconstruction of the former ideal matrimonial and generational micro-story.[11]

Max's micro-stories are based on his memories of the past, which are more meaningful to him than his impotent present. The deconstruction of his micro-stories, therefore is also the deconstruction of an idealized family past — be it in gender, generational or sibling relations. All of them deconstruct the return to conventional family life, and climax in a "homecoming" clustered around Max, the father and Teddy, the returning son, at the end of each of the two acts.

The deconstruction of the ideal family is crucial to the end of each act.[12] The end of Act One is built on a returning son welcomed by his father's embrace (the embrace of the Ur-scene is recalled in the "cuddle" and "kiss"), which is deconstructed in a prolonged dialogue about embracing while the two protagonists stand separate. The end of Act Two deconstructs an ideal-family tableau as well as the return of the son, whose second leaving is even more obscure than his first. Each of the two finales is closely preceded by reference to grandchildren - the next generation of the family romance — and these references are deconstructed too. The rhythm of the construction and deconstruction at the ends of the two acts is tied in with the son's homecoming and leaving. In Act One it is the construction/deconstruction of the recognition phase; in Act Two, leaving home implies a possible construction of another homecoming.

Lenny's full or fragmented micro-stories of the past tend to accentuate power and sex in aggressive encounters. He alludes to moral expectations, but the emphasis is on destructive elements. The constructive element is more pragmatic, aimed at impressing others with his active struggle for power and virility, as opposed to the stories of the aging Max, which turn more on a past of a wished-for family situation.

Lenny's generational situation is evoked by bitter, scorning reminiscences of himself as a baby-child in relation to his father. The baby-like hunger of the adult Lenny and his demand for food, his "don't clout me with that stick" (p. 11), as well as his wish to be "tucked up" by his father, construct a conventional, if bitter, picture of father-infant relations. They are deconstructed by incongruity and sarcasm: "I'll give you a proper tuck up one of these nights, son" (Max, p. 17). Despite the deconstructive element at work here, and Pinter's characteristically underlying comedy of menace, they refer to a conventional father/son relationship.

Lenny expresses his attitude to filial relations in his report on the family which "do make up a unit" (p. 65). In this story the constructive approach prevails, but coming at this point in the family history, the destructive element of the dramatic background is dominant. The "empty chair standing in the circle, which is in fact yours" (p. 65) is a familiar conventional picture of the closed integrated family unit waiting for the returning son. There is also an expected obligation to the family: "they do expect a bit of grace, a bit of je ne sais quoi, a bit of generosity of mind" (p. 65) from Teddy as the returning son. It is from this point on that Teddy does conform to his family's demands concerning Ruth's career as a prostitute. This homecoming of his is thus a deconstruction of the moral expectations we have from the pattern Lenny as brother has evoked, and, indeed, from the archi-pattern of the returning son.[13]

Lenny's sexual relationships are expressed in three micro-stories about women, and are aimed mainly at impressing Ruth. He tells two of them at his first meeting with Ruth, in an attempt to win her sexually. The first is about the lady under the arch, who in the end gets "clumped" and whom Lenny considers killing (pp. 30-31). Even in this story of violence there are decorous expressions — "lady", "proposal", "liberties", "criterion", which intimate but deconstruct a normal, organized existence.

In the short interval between this and the second of the micro-stories, Lenny refers to his "favourite brother, old Teddy", who is very successful and "a very sensitive man". Then Lenny tells his second story in a bid to prove his own sensitivity, which might disappear if he is irritated (pp. 31-32). In this story an old lady asks for a hand with her iron mangle. Lenny is "desensitized" and made violent by the fact that the lady's "brother-in-law" left the mangle in the front room, whereas she wanted it in the back room. This story, with all its hints of violence and sex, intended to impress and frighten Ruth, is set in a frame of conventional moral expectations. It has Lenny volunteering for "snow-clearing for the Borough Council" and giving an old lady a helping hand. Here, as in Lenny's first story, the moral decorum is mainly deconstructed within the story itself. but also aimed to impress Ruth — the goal of his third story as well. In this — "I bought a girl a hat once" (p. 57), his gallant behaviour is aimed at showing how well he can provide for the women in his life. This hints forward at the provisions he will later make for Ruth (pp. 76 ff.). Her reaction is positive: "I was a model for the body" (p. 57).

Ruth, too, tells a micro-story. Unlike those of Max and Lenny, hers does not relate to a family situation, and is not based on assertion of power and/or sex. She uses her story to hint at her willingness to serve once again as a "model".[14]

Elements from both Lenny and Max's micro-stories permeate the rest of the play.[15] These are used in various ways, functioning as "strings" of plot, characterization and wishful thinking. The epistemological deconstruction of the play is made even more evident by the exclusion of contextual information and by the displacement and transferring of the "strings". A few examples might highlight the function of this device.

In Lenny's story about the "lady" under the arch, he notices that she was "falling apart with the pox" (p. 30). When Max meets Ruth, he proclaims "we've had a stinking, pox-ridden slut in my house all night" (p. 41). The result of this repetition is a blurring of the specific counters of every *persona,* but it evokes an association between Ruth and the "lady".

The next example concerns an overlapping of plot situations. Sam is passive, retreating from any involvement in situations charged with sex and violence. MacGregor and Jessie were in the back of his car, yet he seems to take no interest in "banging away at your lady customers" (p. 41). This same passive attitude is displaced to the "lady" episode, when "the chauffeur would never have spoken. He was an old friend of the family" (p. 31).

Strings connected to wishful thinking are transferred from one character to another. The reaction of Lenny to Ruth's and Teddy's visit to Venice is that "I've always had a feeling that if I'd been a soldier in the last war — say in the Italian campaign — I'd probably have found myself in Venice" (p. 30). The Venice string appears again when Teddy tries to remind Ruth of their supposedly happy experience there: "I took you there.

I can speak Italian" (p. 55). Ruth reacts by connecting the city with war (p. 55). Venice, as a symbol connoting both violence and sex, is therefore expressed in the wishful thinking of several characters, blurring both their integrity and the differentiation between fantasy and reality.

The deconstruction process as a strategy of the play is even evident in its title, which presents us with an obvious problem: who is the ultimate homecomer? This problem is manifest in the play, demonstrated through variations of situations and verbal themes. The two strangers claiming to be homecomers are Teddy and Ruth. They prefer to express their homecoming in variations of action, less so of talking. Teddy chooses to be detached, to "observe" the family and not to act. Ruth is pragmatic and calculates every move so as to benefit from the family situation.

Teddy does not tell stories about relationship with the family, but the return to his home meets some of the expectations of the returning son. He has a key, and expects to find his room and bed as they had been: "Nothing changed. Still the same" (p. 22).[16] Furthermore, he wishes to confirm the expectations he has of his family: "They're very warm people, really. Very warm. They're my family. They're not ogres" (p.23). Thus, his expectations seem to be constructed on the tokens of the archi-pattern of the returning son. His expectation of being received by his father is echoed by expressions the latter uses which connote Biblical father-son relations: "But you're my own flesh and blood. You're my first born" (p. 49).

But the pattern of the returning son is deconstructed by the enigma of the reasons for Teddy's leaving, and the dubious motivation for his return. This comes to a peak in the final act, when he agrees to leave Ruth to prostitution and return to his sons and his career in America. Critics have attempted variously to understand both his return and his desertion of Ruth. These may be a calculated move to end a failed marriage;[17] or (pointing to the fact that he leaves his family again in the end) the final regressive act of a passive personality;[18] or the act of a calculating villain who aims to repay his family in their own terms;[19] or he may be a *pharmakos* figure, to be sacrificed in a ritual to re-establish basic family relations.[20] All these interpretations are possible if they are seen as aspects of a deconstructive scheme. But all are feasible only if measured on a scale of conventional expectation, and this scheme itself is open here to different interpretations, as well as audience reception.[21]

The deconstructive elements brought to bear upon the returning son could lead us towards another possibility, that the homecoming is a diffuse longing for a state of being, which applies to Teddy and Ruth but could equally apply to the aspirations of the other characters.[22] Teddy states, "I was born here" (p. 22), and he is echoed by Ruth: "I was born quite near here" (p. 23). Ruth's homecoming might be viewed as coming back to her former self, that of a frustrated woman exchanging her secondary role as a professor's wife in a "clean" American academic community for a "dirty" (p. 55) but vivid life in London.

The blurring of the coherent and normative generational family, including the father, the returning son and the envious brotherly relationship, is further blurred by a repetitive strategy. Max is one of three sons whose memory-stories deconstruct his supposedly loving and responsible family relationships, and he pursues an envious bitter combat with his brother Sam. In his own family he lives with a dubious memory of a wife and mother, an envious relationship among his three sons and an unclear situation around the leaving and returning of the oldest son. Many elements of his situation are repeated in Ted's situation with his wife and three sons. These analogical patterns emphasise the homecoming of all of them.

The prodigal son of the archi-pattern is deconstructed in this play. The "homecoming" of Teddy and Ruth is part of a deconstruction of a family ideal, and the focus is squarely on the family.[23] Returning home is ironic. It takes on a broader, more existential connotation, effectively becoming a "state of being". Homecoming is an eternal, recurrent rite of transformation without a stage of equilibrium in which man can ultimately come home to himself.

Yet it may also be argued that the deconstruction of the family ideal is not the end of the story here. A process of "reconstruction" of the need for family life can be seen taking place. This will be explored more fully in the Conclusion.

INDIVIDUAL EXISTENCE AND CYCLIC RETURN:
BURIED CHILD

"What's the meaning of this corn, Tilden?"

Three of Shepard's plays are categorised as being realistic and are called his "Family Trilogy". These are: *Curse of the Starving Class* (1975), *Buried Child* (1978) and *True West* (1980). The first two deal with relationships between generations. Both, like many other plays on the subject, focus on the return of the son (or the father) to his home.

In *Buried Child* five sons return to their home: Tilden, who has returned from his wanderings; Ansel, who has returned from the oblivion of death as a memorial statue; Vince, son and grandson, who arrives at the homestead and wants to be accepted by his family because "it's my heritage" (p. 84); and the buried child of the title who also "wanted to be a part of us" (p. 124). This buried child is very much present in the mind of the family throughout the play, and returns home as a corpse at the end. Bradley, another son, is the one who stayed home, and aggressively expresses his grudge against his returning brothers and against Dodge, his father. Beside these characters from the archi-pattern, there are also, as in other literary versions of the pattern, two woman figures: the Mother, and the young woman, named Shelley, accompanying Vince who claims the house to be "mine" (p. 110).

This constellation of characters also bears other features which more explicitly suggest the Ur-scene. Dodge has affective relationships with his sons (father/son), and there are outbursts among the brothers (brother/brother). There are also elements in the play which recall plot segments of the Ur-scene. Tilden has been to jail during his "twenty years" (p. 71) wandering, and "got himself into bad trouble". Like the prodigal of the archi-pattern, he has "sinned", and subsequently returns home to work on his father's farm. Ansel is the "dead" son commemorated by a plaque and a statue. Even when he was still alive, he "felt like a corpse" (p. 74) when his mother kissed him. Ansel, like the prodigal, is drawn to "a witch" (p. 74), reminiscent of the harlots of the Ur-scene mentioned by the older brother. The buried child, too, obviously suggests "this my son was dead". Vince's return his demand for acceptance in the family and their apparent lack of recognition of him emphasise the "recognition" segment. The element of mystery connected to the child's birth, death and burial — "a pact between us" (123) — functions as the "secret" plot segment.

The guilt/innocence thematic aspect is not connected to any one character. It remains, however, a central theme in the play, and is epitomised by the buried child. The inward/outward return here is diffused among all four sons, and the parallels to life/death pattern, as mentioned above, likewise informs much of the play.[1]

Formal aspects in this play, some of which are characteristic of Shepard dramas, will help to shed light on the relationship the play has with plot segments and thematic aspects of the prodigal son archi-pattern. These elements are: the discontinuity and shifting horizon of expectation; a system of myth and ritual at a deep level of the structure (the fertility myth of the "corn king" and elements of the American myth); and, the importance of the theatrical presentation of the text for the dramatic discourse to be "read".

Within the structure of the play's plot, and also in the way the characters are presented, there is an oscillation between stable and unstable elements. This creates a rhythm which moves between confirmation and contradiction of the mimetic referentiality. The dramatic discourse, in its theatrical presentation, gives meaning to the contradictory elements by use of a mythic mould. K. Eilam's three planes of dramatic discourse are useful analytical tools here.[2] These are: the external actions of the characters, limited to the physical sphere only (level A); the addition of a fictional purpose to these actions, which gives them cause and intention (level B); which is linked, generally to the overall meaning of the text (level C). In this play, at level C myth is used as a uniting meaningful element. The twisting of certain elements of the myth makes the meaning of the play ambiguous and ironic.

The concrete dramatic action, that is, iconic and objective events and figures on the stage (level A), is bereft of cause and intention (level B) but is loaded with general meaning by its tie to aspects of a mythic structure (level C). The gaps left by the lack of level B are "plugged" with mythical codes. The focus of the mythical coding in the theatrical language of the play supplies a framework of meaning which is based on the inherent tension between cyclic continuity and fragmented detatchment in human life.

Tension of this kind is considered by Levi-Strauss as binary oppositions, recognizable in the themes of kinship structure. He termed it "overvaluation" and "undervaluation" of kinship ties, incest representing "overvaluation" and parricide or infanticide representing "undervaluation".[3] This definition is based on opposites: on the one hand, the urge for cyclic renewal, continuity and fertility, and on the other, jealousy and compatibility between generations which breaks out in violence and leads to extermination and death. The archi-pattern of return of the son to his home and his family oscillates between the urge to belong and continue the family, and the fear of not being recognized, ignored or rejected by the family. This nonrecognition may be accompanied by violence and even inter-generational murder.

Within this play the two opposites exist — the urge for continuity and belonging, which manifests itself in implied incest ("overvaluation") and the impulse towards estrangement, detachment and annihilation ("undervaluation"). Hints of them emerge at various levels of the play: the cosmic (seasons, growth and withering); the collective-national (the American myth of wandering, the family and the family farm, baseball and hero-worship); and the family-personal (father/son/brother, birth and death). These levels also connect with the myth of the "corn king", his castration, death and return, in nature as in the family; and also with the prodigal son who wanders across America and yearns to return to his farm and his family.[4]

The mythical coding has a central function in the play. As mentioned, the referential mode of the play is distorted by suspending the comprehension of relevant elements of the plot and characterization, but the gaps left are "plugged" by a mythical perspective, which constructs an alternative code of discourse. The main signifying process of the mytheme is a constant reference to cyclic processes and to the prodigal son as part of this cycle. In this signifying process "overvaluation" and "undervaluation" are dominant in kinship relations, and other segments of the prodigal son pattern are woven in: return, eagerness to belong, rivalry and abundance. From this perspective the gaps in the realistic mode become irrelevant; their very flexibility and vagueness point to the dominance of the mythical coding. Not one son, but an overlapping chain of sons, returns home; parenthood is constantly on the agenda; incest was probably committed, or at the very least intended (Halie and Tilden, and Bradley's attempted rape of Shelly); sons are dead or murdered (Ansel and the buried child). This fluid discourse ends with death (of Dodge, but also the fact that the buried child is dead), which is linked to return to the family and re-establishment on the family homestead (Vince). As we shall find, this mytheme has a further dimension in that it is permeated throughout by an underlying feeling of ambiguity and/or irony.[5]

Roland Barthes claims that there are three possible readings of the mythic.[6] The first is characterized by focussing on an empty mythic signifier which may be filled with basic concepts and creates a simple, unambiguous symbolic framework. In the second reading, a loaded signifier emerges: form and content can be discerned by the twists and tensions between them, and they create an unravelling of the meaning of the mythic signifier, which becomes a pretence — the myth as "alibi". In the third reading the mythic signifier cannot be unravelled because it is an entity, and this gives rise to a dynamic meaning, which is rooted in the immanent ambiguity of the myth itself.

In *Buried Child* the mythic structure may be analysed in terms of Barthes' second and third readings. The second reading occurs when the contradictions in referentiality are given supposed meaning by the addition of mythic material. The subsequent combination of the mythic content with the form of the theatrical discourse itself further exposes the myth as an "alibi". The third reading emerges when ambiguity exists beyond the form and content and extends into the immanent nature of the myth itself, which contains inherent contradictions springing from its own internal polarity.[7] This polarity is evoked by elements of overvaluation or undervaluation in the mythical cycle.

These readings may be illustrated by an analysis of one typical episode — Tilden bringing in the corn (p. 70) and covering Dodge in its husks (p. 81). Halie wonders at what is happening: "What's the meaning of this corn, Tilden?" (p. 75). The instability of the realistic referentiality in this episode is expressed by the denial of the possibility of corn growing: "there's nothing out there!" (Dodge, p. 69), as well as in the seeming lack of reason in covering Dodge with the husks. However, the dramatic and theatrical emphasis given to Tilden's activity, occupied with the corn, stresses the ambiguous mythical meaning here: the connection to the burying of the Corn King, the return of the son and the renewal of the cycle of fertility.

The dramatic discourse of the episode may be interpreted according to Barthes' second reading. There is a tension between the content of the myth, which is "serious", and its theatrical presentation, which evoke irony. The old father-figure is the vital figure here, set against a son who is feeble-minded and helpless. The burial of the Corn King, then, is a dubious signifier of the cycle of fertility — an "alibi". It does not produce a stable meaning to cover overt contradictions, and this points to an underlying core of irony. This corn scene might be taken as a meaningful paradigm for the play as a whole.

This irony is heightened by the immanent content of the myth itself (the third reading). The contradiction here is that the Corn King must die, paradoxically, in order to live, and in order for life itself to be and continue. In human terms, this expresses itself as an unwillingness to die (Dodge) and give in to the continual cycle of death and rebirth (the returning son/grandson).

As a continuation of the ironic reading of the myth, which is based on the gap between form and content, then, there is in the play a tension between the poles of over- and undervaluation in the myth itself (life/death, incest/murder). This tension is particularly noticeable in the way how each generation in the play fights for its position and struggles for its place, unwilling to participate in the cycle. The use of the prodigal son archi-pattern, which is based on a cyclic myth, heightens this ironic opposition. In defiance of expectations, the father fights for his vitality and holds on to his place in the cyclic pattern, at home and within his family, and refuses to let his returning sons take over.

So both the second and the third readings are present in *Buried Child*. They may also be observed in the plot structure, the characterization, and the staging, which all include elements of the archi-patterns of the returning son.

The identity of the returning son, his origins, and his return are placed in mimetic doubt. There are internal contradictions and uncertainty regarding who is whose son. Tilden claims "I had a son once but we buried him" (p. 92). Dodge, however, insists that this is not possible because "That happened before you were born! Long before!" (p. 93). On another occasion, Tilden says that this son belonged to Dodge:

> We had a baby. (motioning to Dodge). He did. Dodge did. Could pick it up
> with one hand. Put it in the other. Little baby. Dodge killed it (p. 104).

and thereafter Dodge seems to assign the child, once more, to Tilden:

> It wanted to pretend that I was its father. She wanted me to believe in it. Even
> when everyone around us knew. Everyone. All our boys knew. Tilden knew
> (p. 124).

The uncertainty of the whole issue of paternity in the play receives an additional twist when Dodge declares of Bradley, "he is not my flesh and blood" (p.76).

The reason for the sons' "return" too is blurred by lack of rationality and consistency. Tilden may have returned because he was expelled from Mexico and/or because he was lonely and/or because he has a continuing infantile dependence on his parents. He has a dual identity: the father whom Vince sought and a son who left, sinned and returned. This vagueness of reasons for leaving and returning is further accentuated by Vince, the grandson. The length of his absence, and the reasons for it, are not at all clear. The reason for his return is presented (by Shelly) as his desire for family continuity. But this intention, presented as an act of choice, is expressed in a return which is full of contradictions, containing and causing instability. The return of the son is also expressed in Halie's remembrances of Ansel, which she tries to implement concretely as a monument, statue or plaque.

The identity, origins, and return of the sons, then, remain obscure. But although interpretations are diverse, and we cannot infer an intelligible sense implying realistic referentiality, the mythical cycle of return is obvious.

In the version of the "recognition" segment, for example, the acceptance or rejection of the son is primarily linked to Vince. His family do not see him as their son/grandson and even ignore him (except for Halie). Dodge, the grandfather, turns to Vince calling him Tilden and Tilden ignores Vince's presence completely, despite Vince's plea to return to his embrace. Vince states his identity once again — "I haven't changed that much" (p.

95) — and restates his memory of the house and the yard, though Shelly asks "Yeah, but do you recognize the people?" (p. 90). In Act Three the leaving/return, estrangement/ recognition patterns reverse when a drunken Vince breaks into the home. He enters as the conquerer, tearing the screen door of the house with battlecries, sound effects and talk of territorial conquest and hostages. It is as if he is a soldier returning from war, trying to renew his acquaintance with his family, which has become strange to him. In this section, it is he who is not sure of his family's identities, or indeed his own: "Who? What? Vince who? Who's that in there?" (p. 125). The internal contradictions in the mimetic referentiality of recognition are further emphasised when Shelly, the stranger, claims a place in the family and identifies the house as her own: "The feeling that nobody lives here but me" (p. 110). But despite the distorted signifiers, there is an emphasis on the prodigal "recognition" segment of the son archi-pattern. Yet this segment is further distorted by its lack of clear target followed by its reversal, the son not recognizing the family.

The lack of recognition, which is closely tied to the inability to find a stable identity, leads us to the central "secret", of the buried child.[8] The birth and death of this child give the play its title and are its main enigma. The paternity of the child and the circumstances of its death and burial — in fact, its whole existence — are dogged with contradictions. Is the child Dodge's, or was it born out of an incestuous relationship between Tilden and Halie? Just as the child's origins are dubious, so is the identity of its murderer. The birth and death of the child, however are, closely related to the two father-figures in the play, Dodge and Tilden. The "secret" and the shame of it is what holds the family together, and this remains as true at the end of the play as at the beginning. The revelation of the secret, the exhumation of the child from the depths of the earth, does not solve any riddle, nor does it place any blame.

The real "secret" remains buried: the plot segments of "return" only have relevance in terms of the myth of the return (from the prodigal son archi-pattern) and of the reincarnation of the Corn King (from the wider mythic structure).[9] The obvious disjunction between our expectations (return, acceptance, reincarnation, and finally revelation of the "secret") and their refutation (meaninglessness of the secret, the child's being and death, the son's/father's being a feeble-minded) leads to the mythical reading of the play.

The mythical reading also gives meaning to the unpredictability of characterization of the sons, which contains oppositions and does not sit well with mimetic referentiality. The direct characterization of the sons, and their indirect characterization by other characters in the play, is replete with contradictions and inconsistency. Tilden, who according to his mother is clever and talented, appears feeble-minded and weak-willed on stage. Dead Ansel is remembered by Halie as an all-American boy — a baseball player and a hero. Yet he dies unheroically and mysteriously in a motel room. Vince, who was an "angel" and who kept the family, is revealed as being emotionless and cruel to his family. These contradictions are not presented dramatically as gradual character changes or as a result of certain events. Nor are they revealed as the result of differing subjective points of view by other characters. They are there, instantaneously and inexplicably.[10]

The characters do not just show internal contradiction, they do not obey generational stereotypes either. Fathers and sons behave exactly the same way. Our expectations of behaviour according to age — infantile, adolescent, mature, senile — are negated. Dodge, the father, Tilden and Bradley, his adult sons, all regress — within moments — to infantile behaviour. Dodge wants his "bottle" and whines "You're supposed to watch out for me. Get me things when I need them" (p. 79), and the like. They wail and sob, show signs of dependency, constantly express their fears of being abandoned, and constantly demand attention, warmth, food and protection. Tilden, and Bradley too, react regressively, justifying themselves: "I never did anything, Mom" (p. 120). "I'm not doing anything wrong" (p. 122). They expose themselves to the rebukes of their parents, who demand that they behave well and look after themselves. But the parents, too, can be infantile.[11]

These inter-generational situations frequently become comic-grotesque, expressed as childlike squabbling: "Mom! Mom! She's got my leg! She's taken my leg!" (p.120). The "grown-up" children continue to play childish games of haircuts, or refuse to play with cars because "I'm grown up now" (p. 103). This blurring between old and young and the disruption of the stages in the cycle of maturity again requires Barthes' second reading. The disruption of age, as well as of the generational gap, reveals the seriousness of the generational cycle as an "alibi".

The expected cyclic rhythm is once again thrown into turmoil at the end of the play, when the borderline between generations and between life and death itself is blurred.[12] Everything that was "buried" in the depths of oblivion acquires dramatic presence (Tilden's return from jail, the child "rising from the dead", the promise of Ansel's statue). With Dodge's death, Tilden and Bradley should inherit, but do not. The inheritance is taken from Bradley and only trivial items pass to Tilden. The main body of the inheritance — the land and "the house...all the furnishings, accoutrements and paraphernalia therein. Everything tacked to the walls or otherwise resting under this roof" (p. 129) — goes to Vince, the grandchild.

In conclusion, it may be useful, as in the "corn episode" to apply Barthes' second reading to the episode of Bradley's shaving Dodge's head. This scene, which comes after the burying of Dodge under the corn husks, re-emphasises the aggression of sons against their fathers, trying to usurp his place. In other words, we have here an evocation of the cyclic myth once again. But the presentation of the scene is infused with macabre humour and deliberately bawdy symbolism: the son, who should properly continue the dynastic line, is wooden-legged (castrated), and the act he performs on his father, again, an obvious act of "castration", is performed by removing a baseball cap and using an electric shaver. The theatrical presentation points to the mythic core, but it is incongruous. The earthiness of the presentation is juxtaposed with the elevated mythical connotations and this scene is also paradigmatic for the play as a whole.

The concrete and often banal way the myth is presented creates a gap — between the elevated meanings of the myth and the low form in which this meaning is expressed (second reading). This creates an irony, which is further deepened when we consider the application of Barthes' third reading to the play, that of the immanent tension within myth connoting its inherent ambiguity.

The inherent ambiguity of the cyclic myth as it relates to human experience can be clearly seen in the character of Dodge. The central irony of the cyclic return and myth, evoking continuity contraposed with fragmentation and estrangement at all levels of existence, is epitomised in Dodge as the father of the family. His words and all his actions defy any connection with cosmic, social and family cycles.[13] He speaks of the existential pain of phases in individual life and mentions seasons of the year individually, not as part of a cycle. He is aware of, but tries to fight, the absorption of the individual into the cycle of life and death. He sees man's influence on nature as minimal - "Corn keeps growing. Rain keeps raining" (p. 75), and is disparaging of belief:

> Full of faith. Hope. Faith and hope. You're all alike, you hopers. If it's not God then it's a man. If it's not a man then it's a woman. If it's not a woman then it's the land or the future of some kind. Some kind of future (p. 109).

He shuts himself up in his house, his whole world cut off from any external experience or passage of time: "There's not a living soul behind me. Not a one. Who's holding me in their memory?" (p. 112). Though he does brag "You know how many kids I've spawned?" (p. 112), he refuses to admit any sense of family memory, and ignores his fatherhood, claiming, "I'm nobody's Grandpa!" (p. 90). He lives in the present and for the moment: "This is me. Right here. This is it" (p. 111).

Life is meaningless for him — "There's nothing to figure out" (p. 78) — and its essence is diminished into painful existence. He cannot be comforted by the great cycles of nature or of human life, and denies any transcendental dimension. His wish to set himself aside from any kind of predestined cycle is also expressed in what is almost a wish to disappear: "I'm an invisible man!" (p. 68). He does not want to die, and is even terrified of lying down (p. 93), but at the end of the play he is forced to submit to death. This fact ironically restores him to the mythic, the general and the ahistoric.[14] The ambiguity of the cyclic-myth, expressed also in the poles of overvaluation and undervaluation, the possibility of his involvement in infanticide emphasises the attempt to negate the cyclic continuum.

Halie is a sort of inverse of Dodge. About her there are traces of the earth-mother, who travels through the seasons of the year, moving from fertility to barrenness, experiencing an awareness of previous generations.[15] The fact that in the first act she is visibly old, dressed in black, and in the second becomes a woman with a suitor, dressed all in yellow and carrying yellow roses, hints at the archetypal figures of the Crone and the Mother from matriarchal myth. She seems to rise and set like the sun, ascending and descending the flight of stairs. She frequently talks about the weather, the changing seasons, trees and flowers. It is she, too, who keeps the family chronicle: "Halie's the one with the family album...She's traced it all the way back to the grave" (Dodge, p. 112). She is the one who recognizes Vince when all around him do not and tries to make peace between brother and brother, father and son, and to keep the chain of generations intact.

But Halie's character and her part in the plot are also subject to contradictions which undermine her "mother earth" image — Barthes' third reading. The mother-myth is in itself ambiguous, in that there can be "too much mother", or overvaluation. So with Halie the possibility of her incest with Tilden, the classic signal of overvaluation, is revealed. There is also irony in the fact that despite all the emphasis on her motherhood, she can be read as being in fact estranged from her family. She has "an overall view from the upstairs" (p. 75), rather than being downstairs, involved, in the main room. At the end of the play she disappears upstairs once more, and her instructions issue from above like an oracle. Nor does her rather dubious relationship with the priest signal particular devotion to her family.

Barthes' readings of myth, applied to the play as a whole, are supported if we consider two other elements of the theatrical discourse - props and blocking/set. Shepard is very specific about both of these.

The most outstanding of the props is the corn, which also appears in a reduced form as the carrots, brought on the stage by an armful and then ritually cut to pieces. The very existence of the corn and the fact of its growing in the yard are alternately confirmed and denied by different members of the family throughout the play. Dodge claims there is no corn — the last time the yard was sown was 1935. Halie insists that she sees no corn, or any other kinds of vegetable. Tilden holds that it was Dodge who sowed the corn and is now ignoring it. This almost exaggerated focussing on the corn of course only reinforces its presence and its use as a theatrical symbol, pointing to the importance of it in the mythical cycle. In the end, Halie acknowledges that:

> Tilden was right about the corn, you know. I've never seen such corn...Tall as a man already. This early in the year. Carrots too. Potatoes. Peas. It's like a paradise out there, Dodge (p. 132).

The importance of the corn on the stage is that it serves to lift the episodes which involve it out of the frame of language alone and into the frame of theatrical signifiers. It stresses the cyclic nature of growth and withering, life and death. Symbols of fertility (corn, vegetables, flowers) are used in two rituals, symbolising the polarities in the myth. The corn husks are used for burial, and a yellow rose is placed as a funeral flower, between Dodge's knees. Yet corn and flowers are clearly signs of life, of fertility. This contradiction once again recalls Barthes' third reading. It is interesting that the corn, at the end of the play, effectively metamorphoses into the buried child.[16] The parallels are too striking to be accidental. The child, like the corn, rises from the ground, and is carried on to the stage in the arms of Tilden.[17]

Two other important props are the blanket and the coat. The blanket is not so much a prop as part of a milieu, but a symbol whose presence on the stage is not static. It is the focus of repeated arguing between the characters, passed from hand to hand, and its ownership is disputed. It is used as a cover to keep out the cold, but also to cover Dodge's head so that he does not witness sexual violence (Bradley's). It is a robe which confers authority on its wearer, which is why it is the focus of the argument between the sons at the end of the play. Vince takes the blanket from Bradley's shoulders and puts it around his own, and finally it becomes a shroud for his grandfather. Here again, there is tension: the blanket gives warmth and shelter, and confers authority, but at the same time signifies castration and death.

The two mythic areas in which the play operates - incest/murder and leaving/return — are coded on two axes of the stage presentation, the vertical and the horizontal. The "secret" of incest/murder, life and death, is located primarily along the vertical axis; both the corn and the buried child appear from the depths of the earth or of memory. This axis expresses problems of identity which are tied to memories of the past, suppression, guilt and the need to confess. The leaving/return mythic element works primarily horizontally: at the centre of the axis stands the house and the family, surrounded by concentric circles which are loaded respectively with elements from family, national and cosmic myth. On these two theatrical axes the characters perform their rituals.[18]

This structure is echoed in the blocking and the set.[19] The most striking visual example of the vertical axis is perhaps the stairs, which Halie climbs and descends, and which Tilden climbs at the end of the play, as a continuation of the movement which has unearthed the child. The "up/down" movement is frequently echoed in the language; there are references to "beasts from the deep" (p. 127), "secret buried treasure" (p. 105) and "bones in the ground" (p. 112). To leave the house is to "Fall right in a hole" (Dodge, p. 99).

The horizontal dimension symbolises wandering (Tilden, Vince and in a way Ansel) and its place is outside the house. Offstage in this play is inhabited by places you wander, perhaps even ending up in jail; by national myth, by California and Florida, by horse races, baseball games and drives in cars. The house becomes a kind of microcosm, which believes that it has an independent existence, repelling strange elements and altogether sceptical of anything existing outside of it. The only way to come home is by violence and cruelty, like Vince, "to usurp your territory" (p. 126).[20] The most striking example of this is Vince's breaking through the screen door in Act Two, an act of penetration, but also, symbolically, of rebirth.

At the end of the play the two axes meet. The horizontal axis is Vince - his body is in the same posture as Dodge's (p. 132). Tilden climbs the stairs with the child's body, tracing the vertical axis against this tableau. But this theatrical coding is ironic. The external harmony of the two axes meeting is disrupted by the underlying violence within both axes. The child is dead, brought up from the depths of the earth, nothing more than bones wrapped in muddy, perished cloth (p. 132) and Vince's homecoming has been almost an act of rape. Even Halie's final speech is not the hopeful panacea it appears to be; it may be that "the rest takes care of itself" (p. 132), but her advice to submit to the seasons and to generate anew, to "wait till it pops up out of the ground", is rendered savagely ironic by the fact that the most recent thing to pop out of the ground is the dead child itself.

So the homecoming in this play, being approached by different mythical readings and supported by clear references to the prodigal son archi-pattern itself, is in the final analysis rendered ironic.[21] It is riven with internal contradictions, disappointments of expectations, role reversals and discontinuity.[22]

Fathers do not recognize sons and will not cede their place to them and there is a homecoming daughter, Shelly, (role reversal) who subsequently leaves (another reversal).[23] The return of the sons is an attempt to re-enter the cosmic, national and family circles.[24] As Vince expresses it:

I could see myself in the windshield. My face. My eyes. I studied my face. Studied everything about it. As though I could see his whole race behind him. Like a mummy's face. I saw him dead and alive at the same time (p.130).

His attempt exposes the enigma inherent in the prodigal son archi-pattern, as well as other enigmas inherent in related cyclic myths. The archi-pattern appears cyclic and harmonious, but is in fact polarised, seething with internal contradiction. An unambiguous homecoming is impossible: instead, the process of homecoming is diversified, doubted and deprived of any stable meaning.

III. CONCLUSION

MODERN POST-FIGURATION OF THE ARCHI-PATTERN

The archi-pattern of the prodigal son takes on a transitional character in later configurations. After the Middle Ages, mythical and theological emphasis was increasingly displaced by a secular world view. The 19th and 20th centuries mainly presented the prodigal son as the "returning son". This change in configuration is based on variation of the categories by which the dramatic text organizes itself as a pattern reflecting social and cultural codes.[1] The religious framework is replaced by value judgement and the father's mercy by a search for "truth", a truth which becomes progressively more enigmatic. The archi-pattern "loses" its prodigality; homecoming is not a real or pretended act of forgiveness, but a return to a home which turns increasingly from a place of shelter to a state of contention. The modern homecoming shifts the emphasis from the son to the family situation.

The concluding discussion of the modern post-figuration of the pattern deals mainly with the three thematic aspects of the archi-pattern, guilt/innocence, inward/outward and life/death, which have further relevance if we apply them to the six plays as a whole or, as suggested in the introduction, to the clusters of "realistic" and "modernistic" plays. A comparative reference to the theme horizon in the plays will be followed by separate consideration of each plot aspect of the archi-pattern. We have noted that the theme of guilt is connected to plot elements like "secret" and "confession". The inward/outward theme links overall to the problem of age and gender specification, and to changes in the family from a place of refuge to a place of encounter. The third thematic aspect, life/death, is metonymic to withdrawal and "return", or connotes "reception" into a larger, cyclic mythical pattern. The fourth section will deal with textual strategies and elements of deconstruction, and postulate "a new language of homecoming".

The three realistic plays deal with man's deterministic encounter with economic and psychological factors, as well as with the growing denial of the validity of any definite cognitive social premises. The characters in the plays are all haunted and on the verge of losing their identities and dignity: the Alvings by inherited disease and "ghostly" social standards, the Tyrones by their psychological obsessions and torments and the Lomans as victims of a ruthless social reality which destroys their inner selves. An important component in these dramas is the causal linkage among atrocity, guilt and punishment. In the modernistic plays, by contrast, norms are questioned or denied, causing infamy and remorse, and the plays themselves express a deep scepticism towards the relevance of social as well as family categories. They connote a consciousness of the relativity of any value system and growing epistemological scepticism. This culminates in a nostalgic quest for home - an ideal home, which is made up of abstracts that serve for reality.

Carol Rosen notes that modern plays are "plays of impasse", showing an increasing preoccupation with life situations. The protagonists, experience a sense of "entrapped freedom":

> Contemporary plays of impasse tend to focus on the setting engulfing the individual rather than on the individual himself, and tend to find that setting reductive, at once diminishing and intensifying the experience of survival within bounds, against odds.[2]

The realistic plays discussed here tend to be plays of impasse in which the characters, including the prodigal son, are lost in a situation (heredity in Ibsen, failure in life in O'Neill, the impact of social change in Miller) which they do not understand. As a result, they experience "lives not lived". They are controlled by guilt feelings and unsatisfied desires, which they misunderstand, and are finally lost in an incoherent and confined situation. This is most evident in the O'Neill and Miller plays, in which the characters pass life mainly by talking about what they might have done or been.

The feeling of estrangement which was anchored in the psychological and the social in the former dramas changes to one of dispersion of the self in the modernistic. The family members in the former plays suffer from the punitive mores of a social system, but still orient themselves within it. In the later plays, however, the family no longer operates as a successful, or unsuccessful, mediator between the individual and society. The characters are excluded from society and the universe by impersonal forces, and their actions are devoid of meaning. In the former plays, the trapped characters can at least find symbolic referents for their condition in the world which engulfs them, in the later, the referential strategy turns to an inward symbolic order.

These changes in the archi-pattern form variants on the "new language" of homecoming. The former plays are realistic, constraining: the later have a modern, permissive discourse.[3] This breaks the distinction between the manifest and latent content of the dramas, and shifts the emphasis from analysis of plot and characters to the text. The text is treated as a discourse in which our drives become symbols or signifiers and what is hidden or unsaid is "said".

THE TRANSFORMATION OF THE THEME HORIZON

Guilt/Innocence

The unequivocal demonstration of the prodigal son's riotous living, decline, guilt and repentance, and his subsequently forgiveness by a loving father most evident in the Ur-scene, was relinquished with the secularisation of the prodigal son archi-pattern. While a didactic moral premise prevailed in the dramas of the 16th and 17th century, this was progressively challenged and eroded. The implicit belief in a monolithic moral code as one made absolute by the Divine or by the authority of norms was deposed, and the judgement of guilt, and thus of repentance, became more situation-bound and subjectively oriented.

In the three realistic plays, reliance on a code of normative behaviour, causing "guilt", exists but its manifestation is challenged on various grounds: as fallacious and deceptive (Ibsen), as disconnected from the life situation (O'Neill) and as alienating man from his true self (Miller). The son's leaving home as a kind of resistance to his forefathers' scale of values is only indicated by a depiction of the son as having artistic aspirations and unconformist traits (Oswald, Edmund, Biff). It is the lives of their parents which make the children prodigal: Oswald, Regina, Jamie and Edmund are haunted by guilt, and Biff and Happy's identities are diffused, their integrity lost. All this comes as a result of the lives of the children's respective parents and grandparents. Sin is passed from generation to generation.

There are no forgiving fathers, as they themselves are guilty. But there are mitigating circumstances: Captain Alving did not have an outlet for his "joy for life", nor did Mrs Alving understand him. Tyrone blames the drunkenness and desertion of his father for his own stinginess and neglect of his family's needs. Willy is totally bound to idealized, imaginary father and brother figures, and it is they who disconnect him from his family. A metaphorical expression of "the sins of the fathers visited upon the children" may be observed in the "illness" (be it disease, drunkenness or the inability to succeed) which is carried over from fathers to sons.

In the post-figuration of the three modernistic plays, the guilt and repentance theme is further transfigured, distorted and refuted across generations. Guilt is transformed into fear of an existential void, an eternal unsatisfied need for love and communication, and an awe-inspiring death, which is imagined, anticipated or actually "occurs" at the denouement of the drama. Identity is in doubt and communication with "the other" are disrupted. The characters, sons as fathers, move and are trapped into narrow spaces, trying out different versions of existence. They blame each other for not being able to share life, and themselves for not being satisfied with their own existence. The sons, themselves fathers, blame their fathers for having sired them (George, Lenny, any of the possible fathers in Shepard).

Homeleaving and homecoming, as an experience of cyclic movement between life and death but also as an expression of generational needs, is disrupted. In Freudian terms the "totem meal", which was a rebellious experiment, became a "commemorative sacrament", and as such, increasingly ambiguous. The memory of slaying the father, re-emphasised by the 20th-century collapse of patriarchal authority, makes the celebration of seizing the father's power ambivalent and emphasises the brothers' ambiguous relationship. Most evident in Pinter's and Shepard's plays, the seizure of the father's authority brings increased guilt, dispersed and expressed in ambiguous and violent relations among siblings.[4]

Constant accusation between the generations is dramatized, but this is not connected with any identifiable sinful act or characteristic. The identities of the characters is diffused, and stable contextual information concerning events is excluded. Guilt is not defined, but an equivalent sense of outrage, fright and dismay prevails.

The theme of guilt in all six dramas is closely connected to the prevailing element of the "secret", one which covers up some sin and demands repentance. The implication is that the revelation of this secret might be a key to resolve the conflicts of the dramatic present and is related to the homecoming of the son. But the secret reveals itself only as misinterpretation of the past. Moreover, it is not even crucial for resolving the present situation. The importance some of the characters attribute to it is a way of avoiding the torment of the present or confrontation with other characters. There is no clear line of cause and effect; it transpires that Oswald's torment is due as much to his mother's rigid conformity to "ghostly" norms (a fact which she herself acknowledges) as to the "secret" that his father was diseased. The secret of Mary's addiction is fallacious: all the characters in fact know it, but they are in a "conspiracy of silence", hoping that if they do not admit its existence it might go away. The "secret" of marital infidelity in Miller's play is only a cover for a much deeper situation concerning betrayal between fathers and sons.

The secret in the modernistic plays does not relate to any definite event or person. As mimetic referentiality is unreliable, or altogether denied, memory shifts, and there can be no definite secret or secret bearer. Therefore, the secret is illusory, anchored in fantasy (Albee), in an obscure episode in an impalpable past (Pinter) or in a mythical symbol (Shepard).

The secret of George's and Martha's returning son, his birth and his death, does not have any relation to reality except by internal laws of logic and (mainly subconscious) displacement. The secret only exists as a discourse built on the inner desires of the two characters who utter it. In Pinter's play the secrets of the past, as well the present, remain unsolved. The one apparent revelation by Sam of Jessie's past infidelity, does not make the multiple unexplained events of the present any more coherent. The exhumation of the buried child in Shepard is a symbolic version of it. Pinter's and Shepard's secrets do not "solve" the plays; they sustain suspense, creating a tension between anticipatory hypothesis and unpredictability.[5] Thus in the modernistic plays the revealing of the secret only emphasises the instability and paradoxes of events, contributing to the diffuse atmosphere of fright which pervades them.

The "confession" element is also connected to the thematic aspect of guilt/innocence. Relating to past events, whether secret or not, is an integral part of homecoming. In the Ur-scene the thoughts of the prodigal are a kind of inner confession relating to them. The moral scruples of the returning son in the realistic plays are manifested as confessions in soliloquies or in dialogue. As Paul de Man states:

> To confess is to overcome guilt and shame in the name of truth; it is an epistemological use of language in which ethical values of good and evil are superseded by values of truth and falsehood, one of the implications being that vices such as concupiscence, envy, greed and the like are vices primarily because they compel one to lie. By stating things as they are, the economy of ethical balance is restored, and redemption can start in the clarified atmosphere of a truth that does not hesitate to reveal the crime in all its horror.[6]

The realistic plays are still connected with the characters' experience of this type of guilt; value-oriented confessions are interwoven into the text. Examples are the dispersed confessions of both mother and son in Ibsen, the central confessional duologues in O'Neill, and Willy's fantasies in Miller — a kind of inner confession.

The modernistic plays also include signifiers of confession, but the signified no longer resides in the realm of "truth and falsehood", or, indeed, in that of "good and evil". Instead, the implicit belief in epistemological and ethical premises is shattered. Martha's and George's confessions hide more than they reveal; Pinter's confessional micro-stories of supposedly past occurrences are aimed to assure positions in a present combat, and so are the "confessions" of Vince and Dodge.

The implicit concretisation of the guilt/innocence theme in aspects of the secret and of the various confessions, becomes shattered over the course of the six plays. Epistemological as well as ethical stratification become doubtful.

Inward/Outward

Dramas, especially those centring on the family theme, are built on the "between" of personal relationships.[7] However, the homecomings in the six plays discussed here are constructed not only on the inward premises of interpersonal relationships but also on outward premises, between the family and society. The returning son in these dramas is part of a dynasty, relating to his father, mother, wife, brother as well as to his forefathers, but simultaneously the place of the family as a unit in society is presented. The code of the relationships in these dramas can be better understood when some prominent dynamic changes in the modern socio-cultural background are considered. The conflicting trends of turning inward to the home and family as a safe haven and outward to society as a battleground have become intermingled. The plays reflect this change by dramatic metaphorisation of the family as the "between".

The problem of distinction between inward and outward, a distinction between the private and the public, is evident in these plays. The social aspect became complicated after the disappearance of the *oikos* type of family.[8] J. Habermas points to the growing dichotomy between home and work in the modern family. He analyses the nuclear family as having lost its dominant economic function. Its reliance on wages means it ceases to constitute a unit of production. The retreat to the intimacy of the family is not an aim in itself but is caused by the increasingly incomprehensible complexity of the accepted social sphere.[9] Luhman, too, postulates the growing complexity of modern life, and claims that the family remains a relevant social institution even so.[10] One of the results of the modern relationship between family and society has been the development of a gap between childhood and the "real life" of adulthood, caused by the efforts of the family to shield their children from the outside world inside their homes.

In John Demas' account the American family (relevant to families in the Western world) has undergone a transitional process of placement which had three stages. He termed the first stage the "family as community". The second, beginning in the 19th century, was the "family as refuge", which evolved into third stage, "family as encounter".[11] The second and third of these terms are particularly useful here: the family as refuge in the former plays becomes a family of encounter, indeed, of combat, in the later. The family and the prodigal son as part of it are thus a context-bound dramatic utterance, relating to the changing social world.[12]

This social stratum finds its metaphorical expression in many of the plays. Willy Loman does not grasp the complexity of the changing world around him and uses his subjective, outdated world view as a yardstick for raising his sons. Biff, the returning son, understands finally that his father had "wrong values", wrong mainly because he could not differentiate between private and public. George fails to prove himself in the outside world, and this failure is the core of his inner life and his relationship with Martha. Pinter's characters measure their status in the family by their real or imagined status "outside" in "work". Vince, in his aggressive efforts to be recognized, uses forceful images of return which evoke the cowboy or the returning veteran, both images which have special significance as American social codes. A growing disruption of boundaries between the secure family and its norms, and the complex and competitive outside world, moved the combat of the latter inside.

Another aspect of the closing of the gap between the inside and the outside of family life is manifested in the division of male and female roles and in the difference between generations. The family is a primary form of social organisation, in which paternal as well as sex roles are exercised. In the family, individuals are stratified within status and power hierarchies according to gender and age. But in modern times the basic structure of the family has undergone rapid and considerable change in respect of these two main factors. In the sphere of sex, the division suggested by Talcot Parson's structural, functional approach — the "Instrumental" role of the male and the "Expressive" role of the female — has been challenged by the postulation of involvment by both sexes' in career and in family matters alike. The patriarchal system is being dismantled, and changing family systems are emerging in response. This diffusion of set roles brings with it an erosion of gender as well as age identities.[13]

One central change accompanying this has been in the status of the father. This status originally resulted mainly from the split between the productive and the consumptive functions of the family.[14] The father became more and more the provider, and the mother was she who took upon herself the consumptive and socialisation tasks. So the mother had two functions, to be affective and nurturing and the socialising factor of the family. But the father's position became more complicated as it depended on a variable status in the outside world. His social role defined his status in the eyes of his family.

Some elements of these developments are reflected in the dramas of this period.[15] In Ibsen, O'Neill and Miller, the family is a middle-class urban unit in which there is differentiation of gender and age roles. The father has a great responsibility as the provider and the representative of the family in the world outside, and his success or failure is crucial for the family's social position. Mrs Alving hid the truth about the Captain's illness and his failure as husband, father and provider, and she herself took over his role, much to the admiration of others. Tyrone was a family provider from childhood on, and family provision and status is Willy Loman's main concern. With both these men, but chiefly with Willy, the effort to enforce their status as father, husband and provider is emphasised by their concern to be recognized as a success in the family as well as in the community. The children's recognition of their fathers' social, economic or moral failure is a central factor in the inner tension and ultimate dissolution of the family. The legitimate attitude of the returning sons to the father is shattered when he fails as the provider, and his affectional role is diminished accordingly.

The mother figure is the "True Woman", an idealized character who is supposed to be at the centre of the cult of the home. Mrs Alving is such, bearing the double responsibility of the roles of father and mother; Mary is the emotional centre who brings about the ruin of her family, the more so because its other members expect so much from her and are therefore doubly disappointed when she cannot comply. Linda, the mother after whom "they broke the mold", is the quiet, firm and lasting centre of her family, trying unsuccessfully to shield her husband from a devastating sense of failure and her sons from hurting their father's already shattered sense of self-respect.

In the modernistic plays the sexes engage in a struggle for assertion and dominance. Martha does not have an outlet either for her maternal instincts or for achievement of her ambitions, which she has to project on to George. Ruth is "the victim who refuses to be victimised".[16] She channels her dominance in the family through the medium of sexual activity. In Shepard's male-dominated world Halie too is powerful. She represents the cycle of fertility which the men either aggressively have to conquer or submit to in order to achieve resurrection as the "buried child".[17]

The gender roles are diffused, mixing what were previously considered masculine and feminine attributes. Aggression and empathy are not sex-restricted. Martha is disappointed that she has not been able to fulfil the academic role socially prescribed for a son, but George does not come up to expectations in the rat-race of academic life, or indeed in any other sphere. In Pinter, Max finds compensation for losing his outer role by filling the mother position, and even bickering over it with Sam.

Ruth's negligent, inconclusive behaviour as wife, mother and even whore is a further example of this diffusion. She becomes increasingly aware of male domination, and undergoes a sort of consciousness-raising.[18] She resists being confined to the tasks of homemaking, cooking and child rearing. At the end of the play she demonstrates behavioural traits which are conventionally clustered as masculine — initiative, aggression, making a profit, in short, "instrumental" characteristics.[19] It is therefore possible to view Ruth's standpoint at the play's end as a "strategy of feminism", turning the tables on accepted normative sex attitudes. She rejects the accepted dichotomisation of sex differentiation and makes an invasion into the patriarchal structure.[20]

The shift from the family as refuge to the family as encounter is also recognizable in the generational elements of the six plays. In the modern family, the transition to adulthood has become prolonged and difficult.

Home is still a kind of shelter from the outside world, a place to prepare for its complex challenges. Leaving home and returning to it is charged with great tension, alternating expectations with disillusion. In most of the plays the returning sons are not young, in or around their late thirties, yet somehow they are unable truly to leave home. They are still groping for a steady economic and social position and reluctant to have a family of their own. Their identities are in some way under threat and all of them seem somehow handicapped. Their homecoming is a retrograde psychological step, following an unsuccessful attempt to leave the nest and cope with adulthood. In the three realistic plays the homecoming is a belated attempt to seek shelter; in the modernistic plays it is an abortive effort to find the self in a shifting and ill-defined reality. Both of these drives, it should be noted, are presented as adolescent, even childlike, in nature. The occasional lapses by Lenny into "child language" and Tilden's infantile behaviour would seem to support this.

In Pinter and in Shepard the overt generational status expectations are broken. The parents are no longer representatives of a lineage, and they lose the functional relationship with the next generation. The linkage between generations becomes more digressive. A relationship between "equals" appears, and the potential for violence is heightened.[21] The traditional expression of the relationship between equals is, of course, the relationship between siblings. It should therefore come as no surprise that the plays demonstrate various antagonistic aspects of sibling relationships. In the Ur-scene the tension between the brothers was based on inheritance, and the love and status attributed to them by the father. In the modern versions envy and competition between the brothers is based mainly on personal achievement in roles in the outside world, and consequently in the eyes of the parents (O'Neill, Miller, Pinter and Shepard).

So once again we see that a thematic aspect of the prodigal son archi-pattern is put into dispute and becomes progressively more fragmented over the course of the six dramas. The inward/outward theme is linked to broader issues of gender and age and the relationship of the individual to society as a whole.

Life/Death

The prefiguation of the life/death thematic aspect was connected with the concept of sin emphasised in the religious Ur-scene. The return of the son from a sinful life was expressed by the father as "He was dead and has come to life", and the return home was a state of being "found", a return to a righteous existence. In modern drama, however, death, or the threat of imminent death, comes as an ending to an unsuccessful return. This return can be made by sons, or by fathers as sons, and is not linked to a choice between sin and repentance. This shift of the meaning of life and death from an ethical choice to an existential state varies in the six plays.

In the realistic plays, the link between sin and death is distorted. The sons do not sin, but they inherit the cause of their death from their forefathers: Oswald's disease, Biff's failure. However, the visitation of the sins of the fathers upon the children is not direct. Alving's frivolity, Tyrone's stinginess and Willy's view of life are all motivated and to some extent justified. They therefore lose their moral impact as sins, and the linkage between death and being "lost" is broken.

In the modernistic plays death is even further removed from any linkage to moral choice, be it of fathers or of returning sons. Moreover, death is not necessarily clinical, it is often a process of slow decline, a sort of death-in-life. The boundary between the two states is blurred. This state is most evident in the characters of Max, Sam and Dodge. The "death" of Sam and Dodge, at the end of the respective plays, is not even presented as certain. Both characters look dead, but their departure from life has no particular impact and does not elicit any kind of predictable reaction from the characters around them. Max is "reduced" to a doddering, powerless father-figure trapped into a permanent state of submission.

One known phenomenon of modernism is that the more references to the real are challenged, the more mythical elements invade the rendering of existence. These elements are set in an "inhospitable environment" — rational references to the real in the realistic plays, the evocation of tension, doubt and irony in the modernistic.[22] The rhythm between life and death, and the growing referential indistinction between the two states over the development of the plays seem to point to a problematic rhythm between the periods of human life. All the dramas deal with three generations, connoting an additional life/death element. This rhythm of life and death is tied to the inclusion of elements from the cyclic process in the dramatic strategy. This mythical element varies among the plays, and is at its most evident in Shepard, where it is a crucial part of the play's entire metaphoric mode.

The circular links which inform the prodigal son archi-pattern are primarily of death and resurrection. Because, as we have discovered, the prodigal is "lost" and "found", the rituals of withdrawal and return are a version of death and life and of the cyclic process. These rituals are recognizable in various ways in the realistic dramas, where they have relatively low prominence. In Ibsen, for example, the homecoming of the son evolves as a regression to childhood and to death.[23] In O'Neill, Mary might be seen as a sacrificial figure; in Miller, the Pan-like figure of Willy's father and Willy's own urge for death hint at mythical elements. In Albee, the imagined son carries mythical overtones, and is duly sacrificed. But in all these four plays the mythical elements are devoid of a cyclic rhythm of death and rebirth.

The last two plays are more metaphorical, and the discursive practice includes more crossing and recrossing of elements from the cyclic process. But the horizon of expectations inferred from the inclusion of myth — the underlying idea that there is a harmonious cycle of slipping into death or passing into life — is negated. The older characters, like Max and Dodge, refuse to accept the cyclic rhythm and revolt against the inevitability of losing their vitality. They woo their sons' women in a last-ditch attempt at a vital life. Their sons' homecoming evokes their own desire to live, and they will not cede their places.

Homecoming and leaving are metonymic, suggestive of life and death. But the blindness of the universe to man's existence arouses an existential fear. Departure from life is distressing, and the universe is indifferent to it; these are expressed as an act of analogous unrecognition by members of the family of the dying fathers as well as of the live sons.[24]

J. P. Strelka, in his discussion of the concept of myth, sets out three different approaches to it.   One of them is most appropriate to this discussion:

> Myth stands for a statement or concept with which many people agree or pretend to agree, although it does not hold true. It can sometimes be a sort of euphemism for a lie.[25]

So myth here has a deep general psychological validity but is shown to be ironic in its relationship with individual reality.   This is also true of the myth of return which is evoked by the life/death thematic aspect within the six plays.   Any sense of eternal, repetitive return is challenged, and collides with individual existence.   The myth retains its validity, and therefore much of its coding power, but these are reflected and distorted by irony.

THE NEW LANGUAGE OF HOMECOMING

Variants of the New Language

The archi-pattern of the prodigal son in drama changed as a result of social codes and dramatic conventions. The religious interpretation was transformed into a moral, didactic one, and in modern times has gradually become the dramatization of the dubious potentiality of homecoming. Returning home becomes an act of wishful thinking, whose probability is deconstructed in the text, though a longing for family life can be extrapolated from it.[26] The six plays considered here use various strategies to demonstrate a perennial dread of family life and of returning to it, but they still manage to evoke a memory of the family romance, in which the returning son functions as a memory-bearing actor.

A formal summarizing study of the six plays will give us further insight into the "new language of homecoming" in modern drama. This language has various aspects. First, the actual theatrical language of the plays — the words — will be considered. Then the spatial and temporal dimensions of the plays will be treated, with specific reference to the functions of memory and of recognition. This will be followed by an analysis of the plots of the plays, drawing parallels between the decomposition of the plot and of patriarchality, and then by a study of the dissolution of identity, compensated by the element of "acting it out". Finally, all these aspects of the new language of homecoming will be used in a new reading of the modern variants of the archi-pattern, pointing up the difference between what the text says and what it thinks it says.

The Words

The forms of speech used in the realistic plays are inevitably bound to their contexts and other formal aspects. There is mimetic referentiality to "terms of life", the individual's problems and motives within that milieu. The plays consist of logically structured images and contingent linking of plot based on authentic social and psychological elements of reality, and the dialogue is likewise realistic. It takes place on two basic axes: horizontal, directed outward towards problems in the social environment, and vertical, boring into the individuals' inner beings and examining moral and psychological motives.[27] The verbal constructs change between the plays, however, from the prevailing agonistic monologues in Ibsen to a type of interior monologue in O'Neill, and thence to the monologues of memories and expectations in Miller.

In the modernistic plays, as the meaning of homecoming becomes more multivalent and reversible, the architectural pattern of the dramas changes. This encroachment on probability is also evident in the dialogue, which becomes a "dialogue of solipsists" or parallel monologues which show manneristic and parodic elements. Language is denied any communicative function, and reinforces the principle of uncertainty in the moral and epistemological spheres.[28] In Pinter and in Shepard mainly, props (Max's chair, corn, the buried child) serve for lost or diminished linguistic elements, and reinforce the unconscious sphere.[29] In these plays the dialogue begins to take second place to other theatrical elements, and reinforces the "open ending" of the drama.[30]

Spatial and Temporal Dimension

The return of the son is constructed on premises of space and time. Coming home to a confined locality stands in contrast to leaving home for the outside environment. The preference of the returning son for the limited space is a signifier of preferring the "micro-system" to the "macro-system" of society.[31]

In the former plays, the spatial confinement is definite, a preference response to the outside world. The returning son seeks in domesticity the sense of protection and compassion which he misses. In the later plays, the boundaries between home as a micro-system and the outside world as a macro-system become, predictably, more blurred.[32] The home is not a place of refuge and the status of the characters is dependent on their outside activity. Thus they are in a constant state of combat between micro- and macro-systems. George and Martha's home is no safe space but "a dump". Pinter's whole play is permeated with ambiguity with regard to spatial aspects and the motivation for coming home or leaving it. In Shepard, the arrival of Bradley, and similarly of Vince, is an aggressive, even penetrative act. The home is invaded by them and becomes a battleground.

But the dominant element of homecoming is of time and memory. Homecoming is always motivated by memories of earlier times. The structure of the present controls that of the past, however, because every memory is also related to present experience.[33] Homecoming is a state of nostalgia, in which current desires play a part in structuring the memory of events, by distortion, selection, omission, condensation and displacement. The memory wanders back in time to arrive at a place where past events are beautified by current desire.

In the realistic plays the homecoming of the lost son is motivated by the fantasy of reliving retrospective time, anchoring this fantasy in an actual, omnipresent location, the home. His memory of the home as a place of shelter is reliable, but his fantasy is rudely shattered by deterministic events: Oswald's hereditary sickness, Edmund's diagnosis and Biff's "inherited" inability to succeed. In the modernistic dramas, however, memory is an unreliable factor, and the sons' efforts to translate their memories into reality constantly fail. This fight over memories becomes a dominant structural element in these plays, superseding the elements of place, real time and shared memory which hold the realistic plays together. The clash of family memory with the son's means that the returning son must be "recognized" — a sort of Aristotelean *anagnoresis* (the movement from ignorance to awareness). The process of recognition in the three later dramas is complex. In Albee, conflicting "memories" of the imaginary son and his appearance are an important, integral part of the combat; in Pinter, the withholding and deliberate delaying of signs of recognition are a central aspect of the enigma of the play. In Shepard, the avoidance of recognition emphasises the avoidance of all logically structured images of persons and events.

These changes in the "recognition" segment thus signify a growing consciousness that reality, as we comprehend and experience it, cannot be represented, understood or defined on rational and ethical premises. Instead, it is based on the fluid and unreliable function of memory. But this is a subjective feature, and different memories are liable to clash. So homecoming is by definition ironic, because there can be no homecoming without shared memory.

The Plots
In the 18th and most of the 19th century, paternal authority was felt to be analogous to the authority of God, or of rational principle. This might have influenced the literatures of both centuries to be dominated by a linear temporal sequence. The diminution of the father-figure in the 20th century subsequently led to the breakdown of linear plot structure. Plots become ambiguous, fragmented and non-causal, expressing interiority.

The acceptance by the family of the father as the focus of authority and genetically linked descent is connected metaphorically to temporal sequence. Patricia D. Tobin terms the link between authority and plot "the formal imperatives of genealogy".[34]

> It is no accident that the concept of linear time should be as intimate and peculiar an aspect of Western civilisation as patriarchalism: the prestige of cause over effect, in historical time, is analogous to the prestige of the father over the son.[35]

The breaking of this link is clear if we consider the modernistic plays. In Albee, the plot of the son's imagined return is an expression of George's and Martha's interior lives. The linkage of action sequences in Pinter and in Shepard, and the devices used for this linkage, are not obedient to the "formal imperatives of genealogy". Inexplicably violent episodes with no obvious causal relationship to each other are juxtaposed instead. Different children leave and return in a repeated whirl of combat between the returner and his (or her) family at home. Yet there is a unifying thread of sorts, clustered around one returning son (Teddy, Vince), who "leads" the return of the other characters.

"Acting It Out"

The loss of religious or moral essentials of the archi-pattern gave rise to a quest for identity on the part of the characters.[36] The doubts which are cast on the authenticity of characters, or their lack of definition, is a central aspect of the modernistic plays. As Pinter has stated:

> The desire for verification on the part of all of us, with regard to our own experience and the experience of others, is understandable but cannot always be satisfied. I suggest there can be no hard distinction between what is real and what is unreal, nor between what is true and what is false. A thing is not either true or false: it can be both true and false. A character on the stage who can present no convincing argument or information as to his past experience, his present behaviour or his aspirations, nor give a comprehensive analysis of his motives, is legitimate and as worthy of attention as one who, alarmingly, can do all these things.[37]

In Pinter and in Shepard the figures lack the counters of authenticity. Age and sex differences are blurred: adult sons regress into infantile behaviour. Character is enigmatic, and characterization is transpsychological: characters are personifications of various aspects of the human condition. But as *dramatis personae* they struggle to assert their autonomous identity, using the recurrent element of "acting it out". The characters, including the prodigal son, seem to act out and/or direct a scenario of an expected ritual of homecoming.

Albee's play represents a transitional point in this process. While George and Martha are well enough defined not to require role-play for verification or to assert their identities, they do use it to bolster their confidence and exert their power over each other. George subconsciously plays his role as a son, but is consciously a playwright/director in a play in which he also acts the father role. He leads the "bits", alternately playing performer and audience to Martha. At the end of the play, he consciously detaches himself and Martha from the escapist role-play and leads her towards the possibility of a life without play-acting.

In Pinter and in Shepard, however, the "acting it out" does serve a desire for verification. In the Pinter, Teddy attempts to draw Ruth and his family into a homecoming where "Nothing's changed. Still the same" (p. 22). But the script of the ritual play in which he wants to act and direct is aggressively hijacked by other members of the family, mainly by Lenny and Ruth. Lenny demonstrates his characteristics as director and actor in his micro-stories, attempting to convince Ruth to step out from the scenario in which she has "a secret liaison with another man" (p. 34) and act in his play. But Ruth turns the table on both versions of the ritual play — the returning son and the envious brother. She takes upon herself the direction of another version of return. Her play comprises various elements, the daughter who comes home, the wife, the mother and the whore. She directs and performs in these various scenarios, of which only one, or perhaps none, is a verification of her character. Her words to Teddy, "Don't become a stranger", as well as the fact that she wants to be "adaptable", point to her possibly starting yet another version of the ritualistic game after the curtain has fallen.

In Shepard, Vince plays the role of the returning son twice. At first, he acts out the ritual of return, the wish to be recognized and accepted by the family. He attempts unsuccessfully to awaken their collective memory by a series of tricks and parlour games from the past, to which Shelley wryly comments, "They're not gonna play" (p.96). Vince's attempt to verify his existence has failed. His return in Act Two is marked by aggression and frustration. If charm did not work, perhaps playing the soldier will. And to an extent, it does — he receives his heritage. But even so, he is not fully verified.

The element of "acting it out" in these dramas, therefore, functions as an expression of the characters' effort to find not only the meaning of themselves or the world, but also their own authenticity — their homecoming.[38]

The New Reading as Reconstruction

In the six plays the dramatic structure of homecoming as a ritual with underlying rules is grouped around deviation from expectations. The premise of harmonious homecoming is refuted, and disruptive elements become the core. None of the returning sons is received with compassion and family warmth, and to all of them homecoming is disappointing. But underneath the expectations of rapture, and behind the disappointment of these expectations, there is still a yearning to belong to the family as a basic human unit. The complication and fragmentation of norms and institutions only reinforces the need for the family, within which relationships are supposed to be based on "increased trust".[39] Even if these relationships are pretended or violated, they are still expected to exist.

It is for this reason that George and Martha create their imagined son, in an attempt to reinforce their crumbling marriage. Teddy returns home to find a family reduced to outbursts of accusations and aggression, yet still sharing a home. In Shepard, the returning sons have "this thing" about the family (as Shelly puts it), and members of the family hallucinate retrospective, idealized pictures of the family romance. The dramatic discourse presents two contrastive realms: the presentation of an alienated family camouflages a realm of deep yearning for return.

So the model is one of construction (the archi-pattern's implicit expectation of return to a harmonious home), deconstruction (the explicit negation and fragmentation of these expectations) and reconstruction, which is twofold. Its first expression is the hints in the endings of the "open text" dramas that the possibility of family existence has not entirely disappeared: George's and Martha's silent reunion, Ruth's integration into Teddy's family, Vince's choice to stay in his home. Its second expression is the fact of the text itself, of its creation, essence and reception, all of which imply, the perennial desire of man to return "home".

How does all this relate to the prodigal son archi-pattern? Does the construction-deconstruction-reconstruction model constitute a variation of the archi-pattern, or is it a new departure?

Any analysis of this question must of necessity make use of the discussions, like those of Blumenberg and Schöne, on the place of mythical prefiguration in modern literary works. Taking their differences into account, they seem to arrive at similar conclusions: that in literary works *transformation of the mythical* to the literary is dominant (Blumenberg, my italics) or that the functioning mythical themes are a matter of *creation,* not of interpretation of the primary source (Schöne, my italics). So myth is aesthetically reinterpreted to serve the needs of literature.[40]

This is also true of the plays we have considered. The prodigal son archi-pattern undergoes a similar transformation, so that by the time we reach Pinter and Shepard a more creative complex literary schema overshadows the original.

In the Ur-scene, the moral/didactic element is unambiguous. The "question" and its "answer". are presented in relatively simple terms.[41] By the time we reach Ibsen, however, the question and answer, implicit in the archi-pattern, have become more complex elements of a literary scheme. This trend continues, so that when we reach Pinter and Shepard the question is all that remains — there is simply no definite answer. Every possible answer is relative and pluralistic.[42] The archi-pattern has acquired a more complicated literary formulation. The breaking of the commitment to verisimilitude, the juxtaposition of sequences, the non-verifiability of motives, the variety of signification and the multiplicity of meaning lead to a dramatic text which is a composition of the anti-composition. The myths and prohibitions which are expressed partly or fully on the speech level are, in a way, the "obstinate murmurings of language", as Foucault phrased it.[43]

This change is also reflected in the portrayal of character. If we assume that the characters of the Ur-scene are behaviour models, so that the audience is inspired to identify with them and emulate them, it becomes clear that over the six plays the audience moves from sympathetic identification (with Mrs Alving, Mary, Biff, George and so on) to alienation: they cannot identify with stony Teddy or Brad's and Vince's violence. The comfortable myth has become alienating literary reality. So the myth has been transformed, the characters have become alien. Yet the plays still challenge and involve the audience, and consideration of the reason why this is so will lead us back to the idea of reconstruction. It may be argued that all six of the dramas discussed here express the unconscious wish to be re-united with the father figure. The son wants to satisfy the needs of his imagined father and be united with him in the symbolic sphere, since the "real" father has become a deteriorating authority figure. This is not to say that the mother figures are not important. On the contrary, a clear, if stylistic, line can be drawn through the six plays which emphasises the growing importance and complexity of these figures. Put simply, Mrs Alving, Mary and Linda are all vanquished heroines, but Martha and Ruth "play a man's game" and play it well. Halie and Shelly recall Demeter and Persephone, the one an earth goddess, the other escaping, at least temporarily, from the restrictions of Hades.

However, since the modernistic plays tend towards deconstruction, it is perhaps more relevant here to consider the parallel deconstruction — the decomposition — of the father-figure.

As Roland Barthes states:

> Death of the father would deprive literature of many of its pleasures. If there is no longer a father, why tell stories? Doesn't every narrative lead back to Oedipus? Isn't storytelling always a way of searching for one's origin, speaking one's conflict with the Law, entering into the dialectic of tenderness and hatred?[44]

The ambiguous need to unite with the father is common to the reader (the observer) and the writer, signalling a contemporary cultural code. So the play itself is an experience of socialisation between the author and the reader in which both take part in a primary and a meta-discourse. The kinship affective relationships between brothers, replacing the relationship to the authoritative father-figure, are in a way equal to the dramatist's creation of a text to be constructed and deconstructed by the audience.

There is no escape. The relationship to the family and its expression in literature is so powerful that it continues to assert itself even if there is no "father", no "mother", no family to return to. We may argue that the family itself is a "cultural fiction",[45] and that the reconstruction and reception of the discourse of our six plays is based on a fantasy; but this does not take away from the fact that the prodigals we have analysed are still motivated to return, however diffuse that motivation may be.

Any return is, as Bloch phrased it, a return to the hopeful situation of man:

> Something arises in the world which all men have glimpsed in childhood, a place and a state in which no-one has yet been. And the name of this something is home.[46]

Modern drama deconstructs the archi-pattern of the prodigal son only to restate the eternal truth of the desire of man to return.

NOTES

NOTES TO INTRODUCTION

1. On the literary development of the motif and terms related to it, see: Frenzel, 1988, pp. 328-340, 724-744. For a bibliography on the parable in various art forms, see: Kissinger, 1979, pp. 351-370.
2. Cf. Nelson, 1984, pp. 180-181.
3. White, 1980, p. 77.
4. Kushner, 1980, pp. 198-209.
5. Pavis, 1986, pp. 8-9.
6. Kushner, 1980, p. 201.
7. Gadamer, 1975, pp. 284-285.
8. On the form of the parable in the Old Testament, see: Flusser, 1981.
9. Trench (n.d.) interprets the parable in two different ways: either as "the history of the great apostasy of the Gentile world...as in the narrow hearted self extolling Jews", or by seeing in the two brothers "penitent sinners" and "proud sinners", and extolling God's love of both of them.
10. Schniewind, 1940, pp. 4-35, traces the development of the theme on a mainly chronological axis, emphasising its roots in the Old Testament.
11. Jeremias, 1970, pp. 128-132.
12. Rengstorf, 1967, pp. 1-30.
13. Bruce, 1904, p. 294.
14. Geraint, 1964.
15. For other literary approaches, see: Crossan, 1977, pp. 105-141, who claims that the allegorical nature of the parable results in a polyvalent reading;

Funk, 1982, esp. pp. 45-47, who analyses the episodic structure so that the parable may be read three different ways;

Harnish, 1985, pp. 200-230, who presents the aesthetic qualities of the parable based on a structural analysis. For psychoanalytical approaches, see:

Tolbert, 1977, pp. 1-21, who presents the younger son as the id, the elder as the conscience and the father, in his reconciling role, as the ego:

Via, 1977, pp. 21-39, who offers a Jungian analysis in which "the theme of the rebirth of the dead, the finding of the lost, is indicated" (p. 37).

16. Crossan, 1977, p. 139.

17. Brettschneider, 1978, pp. 14-26, discusses an early dissident version of the prodigal son in drama, found in a 13th century Austrian play, *Die Strenge des Rechts,* by Wernher der Gartneaere. The play, which has five acts, has no theological messages, instead emphasising the inter-personal relationships and the father figure, who represents the norm and does not forgive his erring son. The most extensive discussions of the early English version may be found in Beck, 1972, and Young, 1979, as well as in Schöne's article in Kaiser (ed.), 1968. Schöne argues that postfiguration of New Testament sources, when applied to secular events, becomes literary creation rather than figural interpretation (p. 167 ff.).

18. For the development of the motif in the drama of various countries, and for its religious and pedagogic function from the 15th to the 17th century, see:

(von) Stockum, 1958, pp. 199-223;

Schwekendieck, 1930, pp. 1-30;

Brettschneider, 1970, pp. 10-30.

19. Brettschneider, 1978, pp. 27-30, argues that the bourgeois and the rising status of the educated re-emphasised the importance of the classics and the Latin language, for which the plays served as texts.

20. Beck, 1972, p. 72: "The segments of the recognition, repentance and return embody, of course, an anagnorisis, which makes the parable naturally adaptable to dramatic representation".

21. Some discussions of the prodigal pattern in later literary works are:

Camenzind-Herzog, 1981;
Schöne, 1960;
Schwekendiek, 1930;
Brettschneider, 1970, pp. 27-64.

22. The use of the term "ritual" here leans on Luhman, 1969, pp. 38-40. He sees ritual as a chain of expected behaviour in which one act follows another. This type of ritualisation creates stereotyped expectations as to behaviour, which eliminates fear and uncertainty.

23. Young, 1979, p. viii.

24. Via, 1977, p. 38

25. Gadamer, 1965, p. 263.

26. For the claim that Ibsen was the father of modern drama, and for analysis of his influence on English and American drama, see: Dietrich, 1974, pp. 20-34, 71-73, 201-242, 370-372.

NOTES TO DOUBLE PLOT OF THE RETURNING SON AND DAUGHTER: *GHOSTS*

1. Konrad, 1985, writing on the impact of the theory of evolution on literature in the latter half of the 19th century and on Ibsen's work, says: "In spite of the break with divine creation, the idea could easily be seen as a renewal of the biblical curse of the father's sins being visited upon his children" (p. 137).
2. Chamberlain, 1982, pp. 90-91, discusses the connection between Ibsen's works in general and this play in particular and the New Testament.
3. Postelwait, 1976, speaking of the "retrospective method" which characterizes Ibsen's dramas, states that the characters relate to the past rather than acting in the present, so that "the consequence of the remembrance or repression is the central conflict in the dramatic action" (p. 38).
4. Strassner, 1980, p. 13. On the subject of analytical drama and Ibsen's work, see also Dietrich, 1974, p. 33.
5. Strassner, 1980, pp. 16-30.
6. Levin, 1971, p. 8.
7. Krutch, 1953, is of the view that the "ghosts" include three symbolic meanings: the illness passing from father to son, the sins of the fathers influencing the lives of their offspring and the dead ideas of the past, which mainly haunt Mrs Alving (pp. 10-11).
8. Levin, 1971, p. 11.
9. Pavel, 1985, p. 13.

10. Pavel, 1985, p. 17.
11. George, 1975, p. 106: "The conversations of Ibsen's characters fulfil the function of information giving and debate. In dialogue, then, his...rhythm is likely to be attitude rhythm". This is typical of Regina's dialogue.
12. Lyons, 1972, p. 79: "Oswald is the dead child whose function moves from being the promise of a new race to an image of guilt".
13. Cole, 1985, comments on the relationship between Oswald, home and death: "In coming home, Oswald makes asymbolic journey to the realm of the dead, the realm of ghosts" (pp. 79-80).
14. Hornby, 1981, p. 133: "In *Ghosts* we thus see a trio of major characters representing Kierkegaard's aesthetic, ironic and ethical levels of existence". This trio comprises Oswald (aesthetic), Mrs Alving (who moves from the ironic to the ethical over the course of the play), and Manders (ironic). The parallel to Manders' moral deformity is Engstrand's physical deformity. Leland, (1973-1974), points to Mrs Alving's ethical progress as one which is bound to "situational ethics", as opposed to Manders' "essentialist ethics". For more on *Ghosts* and its value systems, see: Bien, 1977, pp. 327-351. Bien asserts that *Ghosts* should be read, along with Ibsen's other plays, as a critique of the value systems of the late bourgeoisie.
15. Brustein, 1962, comments that the dialogues with Manders function mainly as a discourse on norms.
16. These are clichés which take on a satirical meaning through the banal effect achieved by the discrepancy of the speaker or the context into which they are introduced. The terms *Kontaktdialog* and *Kontaktverlust*, as used by Lucas, are appliable here, 1968, pp. 158-159.
17. Northam, 1973, notes the irony in Mrs Alving's wish to care for Oswald as her child as being mainly "for the audience, not for Oswald or even for Mrs Alving yet" (p. 103).
18. Postelwait (ed.), 1984, cites Ibsen's letter to his wife in Rome: "...'the Asylum' for the sake of others. They shall be happy — but this also is only an appearance — it is all ghosts" (p. 217).
19. Northam, 1973, p. 89, remarks as to the dialogue between three characters: "In every instance Engstrand uses fine phrases with

hypocritical intent, but the effect is not to suggest that Manders and Mrs Alving are equally hypocritical; clearly they are not".

20. Kennedy, 1983, states that in the final episode there is an "over determined 'language of conversation' in much of Ibsen's *Ghosts,* but at the end in the dialogue between mother and son...the language itself has something elemental and emblematic about it" (p. 173).

21. Meyer, 1972, also notes the parallel relationships between father/daughter and mother/son. He views the latter as instinctive and linked to primary needs. While the father-daughter relationship is commercialised, the mother-son relationship is based on the instinctual.

22. Leland, 1978, defends Manders function in the play as being based on the agreement that he "sets in motion re-evaluation of the past and [acts] as spokesman for certain central themes" (p.407). But he thinks that Manders internalized these values and ideas, and thus is a tragic "essentialist", not a hypocrite.

23. "The theme of inherited sin reflects the Christian redemption myth, which itself recapitulates the process of neurosis. An ancient mythic crime, an Original Sin, must be expunged by ritualistic re-enactment [of] the Redemption with its numerous New Testament parallels, and its dramatic re-enactment in the sacrifice of the Mass". See: Holtan, 1967, p. 44.

CAUSAL MOVE ANALYSIS FOR OSWALD AND REGINA

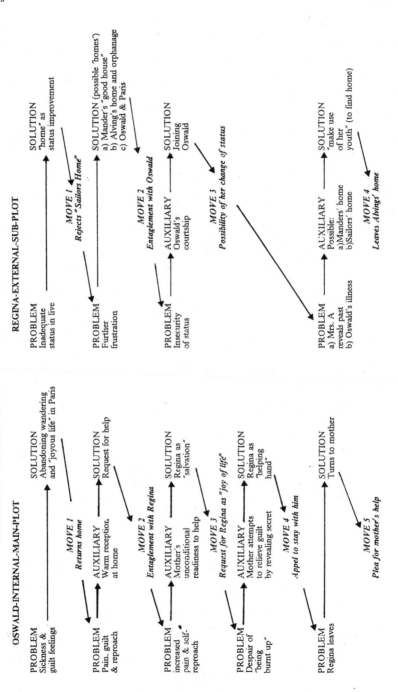

OSWALD-INTERNAL-MAIN-PLOT

PROBLEM
Sickness &
guilt feelings

SOLUTION
Abandoning wandering
and "joyous life" in Paris

MOVE 1
Returns home

AUXILIARY
Warm reception
at home

PROBLEM
Pain, guilt
& reproach

SOLUTION
Request for help

MOVE 2
Entanglement with Regina

AUXILIARY
Mother's
unconditional
readiness to help

PROBLEM
increased
pain & self-
reproach

SOLUTION
Regina as
"salvation"

MOVE 3
Request for Regina as "joy of life"

AUXILIARY
Mother attempts
to relieve guilt
by revealing secret

PROBLEM
Despair of
"being
burnt up"

SOLUTION
Regina as
"helping
hand"

MOVE 4
Appel to stay with him

PROBLEM
Regina leaves

SOLUTION
Turns to mother

MOVE 5
Plea for mother's help

REGINA-EXTERNAL-SUB-PLOT

PROBLEM
Inadequate
status in live

SOLUTION
"home" as
status improvement

MOVE 1
Rejects "Sailors Home"

PROBLEM
Further
frustration

SOLUTION (possible 'homes')
a) Mander's "good house"
b) Alving's home and orphanage
c) Oswald & Paris

MOVE 2
Entanglement with Oswald

PROBLEM
Insecurity
of status

AUXILIARY
Oswald's
courtship

SOLUTION
Joining
Oswald

MOVE 3
Possibility of her change of status

PROBLEM
a) Mrs. A
reveals past
b) Oswald's illness

AUXILIARY
Possible:
a)Manders' home
b)Sailors' home

SOLUTION
"make use
of her
youth" (to find home)

MOVE 4
Leaves Alvings' home

NOTES TO "DUOLOGUE BETWEEN FATHER, SON AND BROTHERS": *LONG DAY'S JOURNEY INTO NIGHT*

1. Other known plays by O'Neill which relate to the aspect of return are: *Beyond The Horizon* (1920, which also contains a returning son and a brother/brother relationship) and *Desire Under The Elms* (1924, in which a father returns to his sons).
2. Tornquist, 1971, p. 42.
3. G.Williams, 1988, p. 9
4. Voelker, 1987, in a recent biographical approach to O'Neill's work, restates that the "family plays" are crucial to the O'Neill canon, and became a central theme from 1913, reaching their climax in *Long Day's Journey Into Night.*
5. Manheim, 1982, p. 4.
6. Cf. Carpenter, 1964, p. 161.
7. Nash, 1975, centres on the home as a motif in the drama. He differentiates between a home and the Tyrones' "house", which has never become a "home" but only serves as a prison for them (p. 77). According to Nash, Mary is for the family the symbol of the wished-for home (p. 79). Her pathetic appearance at the end of the play marks her "homecoming" (p. 83). See also: Scanlan, 1978, pp. 18-19 on the frequency of the word "home" in the play.
8. Cf. Manheim's mention of the motif of guilt and the theme of the prodigal son (1982, p. 6).
9. Black, 1987, sees the relations between the family members thus: "Any stable alliance makes the Tyrones anxious, for any alliance carries the

potential for one to conspire against another. An alliance of two endures relatively longer than one of three, and of them all, Edmund, in his alliances with Tyrone, shows the greatest flexibility" (p. 31).

10. Barlow, 1985, p. 85.

11. The problem as to whether the stress in the play is on the element of the past (Mary and her drug addiction, Edmund and his deteriorating health), or on the developments occurring during the course of the action, is a central issue in genealogical studies of the play. In Barlow's view, it is evident from the process of creation of the play that "Although Mary's readdiction begins as part of a repetitive cycle, the stress is on the uniqueness and even finality of this day" (Barlow, 1985, p. 81).

12. Cf. Kennedy's analysis (Kennedy, 1983, pp. 182-198).

13. For theories of various scholars in regard to the centrality of dialogue in O'Neill's work, see also: Cohn, 1971, pp. 8-10.

14. Kennedy has pointed out that the confessional dialogue of the play is in the form of a duologue: "a community of isolates, a condition of separateness within inseparability. What is redemptive — it is difficult to avoid the loaded word — within such a tragic vision of destructive relationships is the urge towards 'truth telling': the dialogue creates the conditions that allow the 'gradual emergence' into the light of suppressed knowledge, taboo subjects and dark family secrets" (Kennedy, 1983, p. 182). This type of dialogue makes the characters speak "the unspeakable" in their intimate encounter (p. 173).

15. Manheim, 1982, p. 165: "...this play is primarily about human isolation, seen mostly through Mary, and human kinship, seen mostly through the men".

16. According to Lucas, 1968, p. 227, the reason confessional dialogue is to a great extent also situation-bound is because it is always rooted in and driven by the situation. The topic of the conversation is pre-determined and meets the needs of the characters' innermost drives. They are impelled by these inner drives to examine their situation through conversation. See also pp. 182-219, 214-215, 224-226.

17. With regard to the "action" function, note the way that during the duologues language takes precedence over stage action. Bogard, 1988:

"Activity ceases; and each play becomes 'a play for voices' that permits the lyrics of lamentation and loss to be heard clearly" (p. 432).

18. Chothia, 1979, sees in Mary's absence and in the inner, although suppressed, demand for her presence the underlying pattern of the last act of the play (pp. 181-184).

19. On five different uses of interrupted sentences by O'Neill in the play, see: Tiusanen, 1968, pp. 288-290.

20. Kennedy claims that the long duologue between Tyrone and Edmund fluctuates "between the admitted need for companionship and communication" and "angry bursts of accusation and counter-accusation" (Kennedy, 1983, p. 184).

21. Manheim, 1982, p. 173: "What follows reveals both the breakdown of hostility through the appeal for sympathy by the more vulnerable character in a particular exchange, and the breakdown of hostility through mutual affection for another individual, Edmund or Mary".

22. Bogard, 1988, indicates that Tyrone, more than any other member of the family, is capable of love, and when driven towards hatred is unable to sustain it (p. 436).

23. Edmund's longing for death is thus also linked to the symbols of Mother and Sea. As is well known, this play was the outcome of O'Neill's desire to write a series of plays under the heading "The Sea — Mother's Son". "But the characters' memories did form the texture of the autobiographical *journey*: the 'sea' and 'mother' — as both separate and related entities — remained major factors" (Barlow, 1985, p. 64).

24. Cohn, 1971, sees an ironic note in Edmund's statement that he is only stammering, following as it does upon his vivid and precise lyric expression, in which "the sea of mortality relates to the journey of the play's title" (p. 60).

25. "It is as different from Tyrone's confession in its texture as it is in the values it conveys: the inward discovery of a moment of ecstatic freedom in contrast to a permanent sense of estrangement from the world" (Kennedy, 1983, p. 188).

26. "Jamie's confession is the only genuine confession in this play because it deals with life as it *is* more than life as it *was* - which so possessed

both Mary and James in their confession". (Manheim, 1982, pp. 188-189).

27. Cf. Carpenter, 1964, p. 161.
28. Cited from: Barlow, 1985, p. 96.
29. Scringeour, 1977, pp. 48-49: "In *Long Day's Journey Into Night,* the destruction of pleasant illusions about reality is brought about by the forces of good rather than evil. Facing reality is shown here to be a painful but necessary step toward a spiritually significant life".
30. Voelker, 1978, p. 89.
31. Cited from: Cohn, 1981, p. 21.

NOTES TO RHYTHM BETWEEN FATHERS AND SONS:
DEATH OF A SALESMAN

1. *"Death of a Salesman*: a symposium", *Tulane Drama Review,* May 1958, pp. 63-69.
2. See Koon, 1983, p. 13.
3. Parker, 1983, p. 41: "...because the very hesitancies of technique in *Death of a Salesman,* its apparent uncertainty in apportioning realism and expressionism, provide a dramatic excitement..".
4. For an extended discussion of the play, see: Hadomi, "Fantasy and Reality: Dramatic Rhythm in *Death of a Salesman*", *Modern Drama* vol. xxxi, 2, June 1988, pp. 157-174.
5. Levitt, 1971; George, 1975. Levitt regards rhythm in theatre to be the creation of two "change producing elements" which he identifies as "recurrence" and "reversal". George observes that dramatic rhythm resides essentially in the "alternation between opposites, generally producing a pattern of tension and relaxation" (p. 9, also pp. 13-16).
6. Strassner, 1980, classifies *Death of a Salesman* as a "memorative drama" (p. 72), in which the memory of the past becomes a trauma which demands even more than an analytical drama like *Ghosts.* For a comparative study of Ibsen's influence on a play by Miller, see: Bronsen, 1968-1969.
7. Jacobson, 1975-1976, p. 249: "His sense of self-value is dependent upon the response of others. Such gestures of recognition provided signals that society, for a period in his life, was a home for him, one where he might hope to make his sons as happily at ease as he".

8. Cf. Parker, 1983, pp. 43-45; Gordon, 1983, p. 101.

9. Considering the difference between Charley and Willy, Miller, 1965, observes that, unlike Willy: "Charley is not a fanatic...he has learned to live without that frenzy, that ecstasy of spirit which Willy chases to his end" (p. 37).

10. Bettenhausen, 1972, regards Biff and Happy as extensions of two different aspects of Willy: "In a sense the two sons simply continue the two sides of Willy: Biff, seeing the fragility and even the illusion of the vicarious identity which depends on being well liked in the business world, chooses to accept the challenge of a different destiny. Happy, on the other hand, is captivated by the challenge of the dream and bound to the possibility of success" (p. 201).

11. Cf. Huftel, 1965, p. 108: "[Biff] lives heroic in Willy's mind".

12. Orr, 1981, thinks that Willy's turning to adultery can be explained: "the tenacity with which Loman clings to the punitive value of the system, his capacity for constantly obeying, reduce the dramatic space in which defiance can be expressed" (p. 225).

13. Cf. McMahon, 1972, pp. 42-45; Brater, 1982, pp. 115-126 and esp. 118-122.

NOTES TO BIRTH RETURN AND DEATH IN THE WOMB OF LANGUAGE: *WHO'S AFRAID OF VIRGINIA WOOLF?*

1. Paolucci, 1972, sees "the son-myth as the embodiment of that fiction. It is the frustration around which the action of the play revolved". Westermann, 1974, also sees the absent son as the centre of the play. This analysis differs from the opinion of Porter, 1969, who argues that the fantasy child functions here like an actual child in a problematic marriage (pp. 225-247).
2. Paolucci, 1972, p. 53: "Knowing means weaving in and out of irrelevancies and coming back each time to the sore spot; it means indulging in confusion which is not altogether accidental".
3. This summary of Lacan's complex theories is based on: Lacan, 1966 *Schriften I & II;* Lacan, 1966, *Ecrits;* Lang, 1973; (von) Bermann, 1988; Benvenuti and Kennedy, 1986. On the relationship between the "I" and the "other", see esp.: Lacan, *Schriften I,* 1966, pp. 136-137, 143, 299.
4. Lacan, *Schriften II,* 1966, pp. 87-89.
5. Lang, 1973, p. 211.
6. On the unsuccessful attempt to cover up the "hole" created between *besoin* (natural organic needs) and *désir* (desire), see: Lacan, *Ecrits,* 1966, p. 299 and *Schriften I,* 1966, p. 143; Lang, 1973, pp. 227-228; and (von) Berman, 1988, pp. 55-80.
7. Lang, 1973, p. 53: "The Oness [sic] of the self in the other endangers the other with destruction, as he is not the Other and might be

internalized completely by the self. This type of conflict in a condition of coexistence may be solved only by death of one".

8. McCarthy, 1987, p. 73: "The reappearance of the details of this story as novel...indicates how consciously Albee is aiming at undermining the illusion of fact, and substituting a shifting developing *experience* for the audience".

9. Lacan, *Ecrits,* 1966; *Schriften I,* 1966, pp. 136-137, 143, 299.

10. Bigsby, 1986, points out that in the play, illusion alienates individuals from each other. In the development of the play humiliation turns to humility, and the son is sacrificed for the sake of redemption.

11. Roy, 1986, p. 93: "[Martha] is led to recognize that she is a victim of her own contradictory desires, that the world is organized in absurd ways, and that her rejection of George stems from her own father's rejection of her".

12. Bock, 1982, pp. 437-444, argues that Martha functions as an Archetype of the Great Bad Mother in human fantasy.

13. Anderson, 1981, argues that both Martha and George worship their fathers — Martha with admiration, George with hate.

14. Cohn, 1971, notes that throughout the play George is preoccupied with death. All four characters of the play are involved in death rites (p. 145).

15. Schlueter, 1979, pp. 82-83: " The final scene, then, sees a triple death; that of the fictive son, that of the fictive parents and that of fiction itself".

16. Rutenberg, 1969, sees the setting of the campus as symbolic of the theme of Western decline.

17. Fisher-Seidel, 1986, pp. 88-97, finds aspects of Myth parody in the play's different characters. In the combination of George (historical consciousness) and Martha (Mother America), there is evoked a composite American personality.

18. Schlueter, 1979, p. 87: "While it is clear that the games of George and Martha are attempts to avoid reality, it is also clear that games, when formalized into art, are not simply escapism".

19. Roudane, 1987, p. 81: "And the directing force for the metaphysical process is involvement: to 'get at the marrow' means to demythologize

the child, to exorcise the incubi haunting their psyches, to restore, finally, spiritual health".
20. Paolucci, 1972, on George: "He is the double image — both father and son — celebrating in his inspired reading of the Latin service his own death and rebirth" (p. 61).

NOTES TO DECONSTRUCTION OF THE RETURN TO
THE FAMILY ROMANCE: *THE HOMECOMING*

1. Morris, 1966, claims that in *The Homecoming* the set is in fact a family parlour, and that the themes are those which are also favourites of Ibsen-Strindberg realism — Generation, Heredity, Family, Home.
2. Heitman, 1982, pp. 259-260, proposes that Pinter's realism depends on perception of reality. Thus his realism is based on a dichotomic relationship between "primary reality" (emotional and not understood) and "secondary reality" (empiric and known).
3. Burkman, 1986, views this play in the context of other family plays by Pinter, "...in which Oedipal conflict is ritualized into a battle for renewal..". (p. 170). "For the play, despite its seeming cynicism, is about love and about the way the family regroups around the woman who promises it new life even as their needs promise new life for her" (p. 171). Hugh, 1968, sees in Teddy (as in George, in Albee's play) a breaker of our expectations concerning the family. Hinchcliffe, 1967, finds in the play three headings: Family (the bonds that separate and unite), Morality (violent, bloody aspects of life) and Philosophy (Lenny's approach) (pp. 152-162). See also: Vera Jiji, 1974.
4. Quigley, 1975, p. 176.
5. Schäfer, 1985, pp. 238-240, argues that the struggle for power — influence, prestige, authority — is the characters' main motivation. For Teddy the emphasis is on the social role more than the family one; Sam's role in the outside world sustains his prestige, and Max is the only one confined to the family role. Knowles, 1984, p. 118-119: "Yet

in speech and action every family relationship is mocked and scorned". See also: Mengel, 1978; Wardle, 1986, p.171.

6. Postelwait, 1976, pp. 163-164. See also: "The present power struggle, as a social and territorial imperative, is being controlled by the versions of self, which are defined by memory" (p. 182).

7. Kennedy, 1985, p. 186: "The ritualized language of the family lies at the centre of the play and is arranged in broadly juxtaposed patterns of ceremony and its violation".

8. Dukore, 1988, pp. 83-85.

9. Hayman, 1975, writes of the passivity of Teddy and Sam "...it's only Ted and Sam who have any consistency at all and in them it consists largely in the passivity with which they face the aggression of their family" (p. 64). See also: Sykes, 1972, pp. 119-121; Thompson, 1985, pp. 108-125.

10. Gabbard, 1976, p. 195: "They make a tableau of madonna and children".

11. Esslin, 1970, sees the drama as a "perfect fusion of extreme realism with the quality of an archetypal dream image of wish fulfillment" (p. 149), which is centered on the desire for sexual conquest of the mother and embarrassment of the father.

12. Many critics relate to the static element of the play, evident in the similarity of the ending of Act One and Act Two, as well as their ambiguity. Burkman, for example, sees Teddy as a scapegoat and considers all the characters as part of a "double ritual" pattern, in which Ruth, at the end, replaces Jessie and Lenny and Joey replace Teddy and Max. The emphasis passes from the male figures to the female figure, who plays the victim-victor role (Burkman, 1971, pp. 114-115).

13. Dukore, 1988, p. 85: "The final stage picture portrays the ambiguous note on which the play ends". Also, Hinchcliffe, 1967, p. 162: "The real play may, in a sense, be said to begin after the curtain falls; he and Ruth are measuring each other up for the fight that must ensue from the arrangement that the play has proposed".

14. Attar, 1981, p. 67: "Ruth's intrusion signals the liberation of a woman from marriage which has become meaningless". Quigley, 1975, sees in Ruth the victor who has defeated the men.

15. Gabbard, 1976, p. 195: "As the play progresses, an awareness grows that feelings and events are repeating themselves".

16. Quigley, 1975, p. 177: "In the process of homecoming the relationship between change and continuity becomes of considerable significance..". (p. 177). Teddy is interested in continuity, Lenny in change.

17. Anderson, 1976, p. 101: "Eddie, we feel, is intact; and Teddy, the son and brother, has used his homecoming — to liberate himself from his indefinable burden of the past".

18. S.Gale, 1977, p. 147: "Thus leaving home is a classic example of the defence-by-withdrawing mechanism". See also: Esslin, 1970, p. 166.

19. See Peter Hall's opinion as director of the play (Hall, 1985).

20. Burkman, 1971, p. 12.

21. Hudgins, 1985, bases himself on Jauss' theory and indicates that the reception of this drama is based on "a positivation of the negative" in which the audience should recognize that the negative figure ridicules the ruling norm (p. 313). "I term this combination of responses an intellectual identification, dependent first on the thoughtful and then on emotional response to indexes in the text" (p. 104).

22. Morris, 1966, remarks that the "return" to the family is evident in Ruth. The overall result is "restored matriarchy" (pp. 186-187). Hollis, 1970, claims that the men in the play compose "...a composite man in search of the composite woman — Ruth..". (pp. 180-181).

23. States, 1968-1969, declares that the appeal of irony in *The Homecoming* is in its being a kind of pure patterning of symmetrics which have no definite bearing on human ideals: "Thus we might theorize that irony has two aspects: it is, in the moral sense, a defense against the failure of any single option to convince, the loss of a clear stake in an ideological inheritance; and, in the aesthetic sense, it is a defense against the exhaustion of a set of inherited images" (p. 18).

NOTES TO INDIVIDUAL EXISTENCE AND CYCLIC RETURN: *BURIED CHILD*

1. In an interview with Kenneth Chubb, the playwright states: "Death? The idea of dying and being reborn is really an interesting one, you know. It's always there at the back of my head" (Chubb, 1981, p. 207).
2. Cf. also Eilam, 1980, p. 125.
3. Levi-Strauss, 1958, pp. 81-106.
4. For two versions of the prevalent discussion among critics of Shepard's realism and his use of the American myth, see: Skloot, 1986; Porter, 1969.
5. Orbison, 1984, p. 506: "An indication of his dramatic power in his continuing ability to create mythic meanings on several simultaneous levels".
6. Barthes, 1973, p. 128.
7. Shepard says that myth in his dramas "short circuits the intellect and hooks you up with feeling" (Cohn, 1981, p. 161).
8. Wilson, 1987. The spectator is directed to see in the decomposing corpse of the child a confirmation of the "secret" story.
9. Mottram, 1984, comments that the appearance of the buried child at the end of the play shifts its meaning " from a representation of all that is dark and devouring in the family, it takes on the significance of hope" (p. 143).
10. Rabillard, 1984, p. 65: "Shepard employs equally non-realistic transformation of character — absolute reversal of action, or peculiar transferences of behaviour from one character to another".

11. Callens, 1986, p. 411: "In other words, the buried child of the title, Shepard suggests, is the child in each of the men. It is never completely outgrown and keeps hiding in some dark corner of the self".

12. Whiting, 1988, analyses Shepards intention in the drama on the basis of three versions of the play. He concludes that: "*Buried Child* is about a family whose members are 'dead' for each other" (p. 549).

13. Marranca, 1981, claims that in Shepard's family plays the parents are "comic, pathetic, dreamy figures unable to comprehend or initiate events" (p. 16). Yet Dodge here, although he does not initiate, comprehends the basic situation more than other characters.

14. In frame of: "As man, his experience is basically linear, however much he may be, as an object, subject to the effects of natural and social cycles" (Watts, 1968, pp. 127-128.)

15. Callens, 1986, p. 411: "Buried Child reminds us of this original, mythical state of one-ness, a feminine and organic band between man and nature, through water and fertility symbols". Thus Halie, on the mythic-symbolic level of the incest theme, carries these connotations.

16. Nash, 1983, based on *The Golden Bough,* comments that the 'ceremonial pyre' on which Dodge asks his body to be burnt also adds to the symbolic element of the Corn King.

17. For the mythological use of the death and rebirth of the Corn King, cf. Nash, 1983. He sees in Vince the mediating element which, according to Levi-Strauss, 1958, subsumes the two opposite terms of myth: "Yet Vince remains unrecognized because he is the reincarnation of the buried child, now returned to claim his patrimony, a return signalled by the sudden and startling growth of corn in the fields" (p. 488).

18. Rabillard, 1984, sees the "exploration of theatricality" in the centre of Shepard's drama as an expression of America's "culture of theatricality", and also as an expression of "deeper anxieties of modern Western society" (p. 69).

19. Marranca, 1981, p. 32: "For Shepard, space is more than setting — it develops its own thematics rather than remaining decorative, functional or symbolic".

20. Bachman, 1976, sees: "One source of the unique quality and tension in his [Shepard's] dramas in his ambivalent attitude towards violence" (p.

406). He notes that while Shepard's violent characters introduce force, this is defused by avoidance or vitiation of its effect through audience alienation devices.

21. Marranca, 1981, comments that Christian themes and symbolism are an important aspect of Shepard's dramas, and that the interpretation of Vince as a prodigal son is a fairly obvious one (p. 27).

22. See Putzel, 1987.

23. Wilson, 1987, p. 40: "Shepard eroticises the role of the spectator, because Shelly's desire to know the history of Vince's family is ours".

24. Blau, 1984, p. 527: "We can feel in the drama that Shepard wants to undo the double bind, wanting to have it both ways: breaking the law on which the family depends *and* keeping the institution intact".

NOTES TO CONCLUSION

1. Fisher-Seidel, 1986, pp. 25-47, claims that the main difference between American and English modern drama is that while the first emphasises thematical aspects of the American myth (the simple life, self-fulfilment for the individual, redemption), the latter are more tied to conventional expectations. This difference can also be observed in the post-figuration of the prodigal.
2. Rosen, 1983, pp. 8-9.
3. See Pavis, 1986, on the problem of defining "modern drama".
4. Jung, 1969, p. 400: "To take but one example: Yahweh had one good son and one who was a failure. Cain and Abel, Jacob and Esau, correspond to this prototype and so, in all ages and in all parts of the world, does the motif of the hostile brothers...".
5. Pfister, 1988, refers to the point where "low probability becomes completely unpredictable" as the limit of suspense. "Beyond it, the area of tension between non-awareness and the development of anticipatory hypothesis — upon which suspense is based — collapses" (p. 101).
6. de Man, 1979, p. 279.
7. The term used by Szondi, 1987, for drama in general, is most appropriate for family dramas.
8. Cf. Kalkus, 1977, pp. 76-138.
9. Habermas, 1968, p. 18.
10. Luhman, 1973, pp. 13-30, claims that the complexity of modern society and its emphasis on "instrumentality" re-emphasises the need for small

social units (like the family) in which a feeling of "situation control" can exist.

11. Demas, 1979.

12. On the family unit as an institution which partly releases the individual from an overburden of decision-making needed in a complex society, see: Gehlen, 1961, pp. 64-72; Schelsky, 1957.

13. Cf. Hutter, 1981, pp. 327-347.

14. Aries, 1975, p. 564.

15. Konrad, 1985, argues that the theory of evolution had a great impact on the conception of self and human relations. It was, in a way, a renewal of the Biblical curse of the father's sins being visited upon the children, and as such is recognizable in drama (Ibsen). Gradually the question of heredity was formulated into one of responsibility.

16. Kreps. 1979, pp. 50-51, sees Teddy and Ruth as two potential victims who stand up, each in his own way, against being "lost".

17. Sundquist, 1979, pp. xiv-xi, claims that American writers tend to find in the family a model for social and political constructs, which are still problematic for a recently conceived nation. The frontier fantasies took the form of male domination and female submission.

18. de Beauvoir, 1953, p. 301: "...one is not born, but rather becomes, a woman".

19. Eisenstein, 1984, esp. pp. 10, 132-140, indicates the dominance of Talcot Parson's and others' view of feminine "affective" as opposed to masculine "instrumental" stereotyped characteristics.

20. Case, 1988, p. 118: "In other words, the conventions of the stage produce a meaning for the sign 'woman' which is based upon their cultural association with the female gender. Feminist semiotic theory has attempted to describe and deconstruct this sign for "woman" in order to distinguish biology from culture and experience from ideology".

21. Cf. Shorter, 1975, pp. 276-279.

22. Ross, 1981, p. 169.

23. Jacobson and Schoepf, 1967, esp. pp. 44-53, claim that the theme is re-enacted by the protagonist in a way which is different from Christian redemption: "Ibsen conjoined psychology and morality in mythic patterns", (p. 53).

24. Cf. Kolakowski, 1974, p. 93.
25. Strelka (ed.), 1980, p. viii.
26. Blumenberg, 1979, pp. 187-202. The ambiguous and not co-ordinated attitudes towards homecoming may be defined as "Kunstmythos" in Blumenberg's terms.
27. Murphy, 1987, p. 26.
28. Cf. Kennedy, 1983, pp. 200-202.
29. Heitmann, 1982, states that in Pinter's work the stage functions as a "poesie of space" (*Raumdichtung*), substituting for the loss of of conventional rationality, abstraction, displacement, over-emphasis and causality.
30. Pfister, 1988, argues that there are three types of open ending in modern drama: the one where the plot is not "a single constellation of crisis or conflict, but is concerned to demonstrate a lasting condition. At best, it is represented as a cyclic, repetitive process that returns to where it started (Beckett). A second possibility is based on an unresolved situation of conflicting norms (Brecht)" (p. 96). The third is the one which mainly applies here: "There are, however, other texts, particularly of the modern period, in which the author does not resolve even the most basic factual questions" (p. 97).
31. Platz, 1983, sees the character's "preference" and "avoidance" in the spatial dimension as a reflection of man's societal experience.
32. Here the sense of space perceived by the audience is not necessarily the one viewed by the characters, e.g., the house and the corn fields in Shepard. See Lyons, 1987, pp. 26-44, esp. p. 27.
33. Middleton and Edwards (eds.), 1990, p. 41.
34. Tobin, 1978, p. 12. See also pp. 12-29.
35. Tobin, 1978, p.95.
36. Langbaum, 1977, pp. 7-10, sees this type of search for identity taking on the features of combat. Reitz, 1983, pp. 7-37, argues that the search for *essentia* gave rise to the centrality of the identity theme.
37. Pinter, 1968, p. 81.
38. Nelson, 1958, p. 10.
39. Luhman, 1973, pp. 41-49.
40. Blumenberg, 1979; Schöne, 1968, esp. pp. 285-287, postulates that the "repetition of an exemplary situation" (*Wiederholung der exemplarische*

Begebenheit) may be emphasised either in relation to the characters or to the situation itself. The situation-bound use is more common within secular literature after the 18th century. The creative element of the archi-pattern is also mostly situational.

41. Frondizi, 1972, p. 35.
42. Different theoretical approaches could be considered as relevant to this discussion. For example: Gadamer, *Truth and Method,* 1965, demands a kind of consciousness of historicism which preserves the past in our present consciousness; H.Jauss, *Toward an Aesthetic of Reception,* 1982, mentions "horizons of expectations"; Fish, *Is There a Reader in the Text?,* 1980, postulates "interpretive communities". All of these theories are relevant for our argument. The theories of discourse analysis (e.g., Kittler and Turk, *Urscenen. Literaturwissenschaft als Diskursanalyse und Diskurstheorie,* 1977), which state that texts presuppose the reader's view that literary discourse is untrue, may also apply here as indicated in the discussion of modern dramatic coding of "return".
43. Foucault, 1974, p. 18.
44. Barthes, 1975, p. 47.
45. Stannard, 1979.
46. Bloch, 1971, pp. 44-45.

BIBLIOGRAPHY

TEXTS USED

Henrik Ibsen, *Eleven Plays of Henrik Ibsen,* The Modern Library, n.d., pp. 95-177.

Eugene O'Neill, *Long Day's Journey Into Night,* London, 1968.

Arthur Miller, *Collected Plays,* Volume I, New York, 1965, pp. 129-222.

Edward Albee, *Who's Afraid of Virginia Woolf?,* New York, 1962.

Harold Pinter, *The Homecoming,* London, 1986.

Sam Shepard, *Seven Plays,* Toronto (and other places), 1981, pp. 61-133.

BIBLIOGRAPHY

Anderson, M., *Anger and Detachment,* London, 1976.

Anderson, M. C., "Ritual Structure and Romantic Vision in Edward Albee's Drama. A Study of Three Plays", unpublished PhD dissertation, Michigan, 1981.

Aries, P., *Geschichte der Kindheit,* Munich, 1975.

Attar, S., *The Intruder in Modern Drama,* Frankfurt, Bern, Cirencester, 1981.

Bachman, C. R., "Defusion of Menace in the Plays of Sam Shepard", *Modern Drama,* vol. 19, 1976, pp. 405-415.

Barlow, J. E., *Final Acts: The Creation of Three Late O'Neill Plays,* Athens, 1985.

Barthes, R., "Myth Today", *Mythologies,* Norwich 1973.

————, *The Pleasure of the Text,* New York, 1975.

Beauvoir (de), S., *The Second Sex,* New York, 1953.

Beck, E., *Prodigal Son Comedy: The Continuation of a Paradigm, English Drama 1500-1642,* Indiana, 1972.

Benvenuti, R. and Kennedy, R., *Jacques Lacan, An Introduction,* New York, 1986.

Bermann (von), C., "Das Spiel des Significanten. Zur Struktur des Discurses bei Lacan", *Diskurstheorien un Literaturwissenschaft,* J. Fohrmann and J. Müller (Hrsg.), Bonn, 1988, pp. 55-80.

Bettenhausen, E. A., "Forgiving the Idiot in the House: Existential Anxiety in Plays by Arthur Miller and its implications for Christian Ethics", unpublished PhD dissertation, University of Iowa, 1972.

Bien, H. "Das Dilema Spätsbürgerlicher Ibsen Forschung", *Henrik Ibsen,* Fritz Paul (Hrsg.), Darmstat, 1977, pp. 327-351.

Bigsby, C. W. E., "Confronting Reality: Who's Afraid of Virginia Woolf?", *Critical Essays on Edward Albee,* P. C. Kolin and J. Madison Davis (eds.), Boston, 1986, pp. 80-87.

Black, S. A., "The War Among the Tyrones", *The Eugene O'Neill Newsletter,* Summer-Fall 1987, pp. 29-35.

Blau, H., "The American Dream in American Gothic: The Plays of Sam Shepard and Adrienne Kennedy", *Modern Drama,* vol. xxiii, 1984, pp. 520-539.

Bloch, E., *On Karl Marx,* New York, 1971.

Blumenberg, H., *Arbeit am Mythos,* Frankfurt, 1979.

Bock, H., "The MOM als Typus und Archetypus im Werk von Edward Albee", *Die Amerikanische Literatur in der Weltliteratur. Themen und Aspekte,* C. Uhlig und V. Bischof (Hrsg.), Berlin, 1982.

Bogard, T., *Contour in Time,* Oxford University Press, 1988.

Brater, E., "'Miller's Realism' and 'Death of a Salesman'", *Arthur Miller,* R. A. Martin (ed.), New York, 1982.

Brettschneider W., *Die Parabel vom verlorenen Sohn.   Das Biblische Gleichnis in der Entwicklung der Europeischen Literatur,* Berlin, 1978.

Bronsen, D., "An Enemy of the People: A Key to Arthur Miller's Art and Ethics", *Comparative Drama* vol. 11, no. 4, Winter 1968-1969, pp. 229-247.

Bruce, A. B., *The Parabolic Teaching of Christ,* London, 1904.

Brustein, R., "Ibsen and Revolt", *Tulane Drama Review* vol 7, Fall 1962, pp. 113-155.

Burkman, K. H., *The Dramatic World of Harold Pinter,* Ohio State University, 1971.

————, "Family Voices and the Voice of the Family in Pinter's Plays", *Harold Pinter: Critical Approaches,* Steven Gale (ed.), London and Toronto, 1986, pp. 164-175.

Callens, J., "Memories of the Sea in Shepard's Illinois", *Modern Drama* vol. xxix, 3, 1986, pp. 403-415.

Camenzind-Herzog, E., *Robert Walser - eine Art verlorenen Sohn*, Bonn, 1981.

Carpenter, F. J., *Eugene O'Neill*, New York, 1964.

Case, S-E., *Feminism and Theatre*, Hampshire and London, 1988.

Chamberlain, J. S., *Ibsen: The Open Vision*, London, 1982.

Chothia, J., *Forging a Language: A Study in the Plays of Eugene O'Neill*, Cambridge, 1979.

Chubb, K. and others (Interview), "Metaphors, Mad Dogs and Old Time Cowboys", *American Dreams. The Imagination of Sam Shepard*, B. Marranca (ed.), New York, 1981.

Cohn, R., *Dialogue in American Drama*, Bloomington and London, 1971.

————, "Sam Shepard: Today's Passionate Shepard and his Loves", *Essays on Contemporary American Drama*, H. Bock and A. Wertheim (eds.), Munich, 1981.

Cole, S. L., *The Absent One*, Pennsylvania State University, 1985.

Crossan, J. D. (ed.), "Polyvalent Narration", *Semeia 9*, University of Montana, 1977.

————, "A Metamodel for Polyvalent Narration", ibid., pp. 105-141.

Demas, J., "Images of the American Family: Then and Now", in *Changing Images of the Family*, V. Tufte and B. Myerhoff (eds.), New Haven and London, 1979, pp. 43-60

Dietrich, M., *Das Moderne Drama*, Stuttgart, 1974.

Dukore, B. F., *Harold Pinter*, London, 1988.

Eilam, K., *The Semiotics of Theater and Drama*, London and New York, 1980.

Eisenstein, H., *Contemporary Feminist Thought*, London and Sydney, 1987.

Esslin, M., *The Field of Drama*, London and New York, 1987.

————, *The Peopled Wound: The Plays of Harold Pinter*, London, 1970.

Fish, S. *Is There a Text in This Class?* Cambridge, Mass and London, 1980.

Fischer-Seidel, T., *Mythenparodie in modernen Englischen und Amerikanischen Drama*, Heidelberg, 1986.

Flusser, D., *Die Rabinischen Gleichnisse unde der Gleichnisserzähler Jesus*, Bern, 1981.

Foucault, M., *Die Ordnung des Diskurses*, Munich, 1974.

Frenzel, E., *Motiv der Weltliteratur,* Stuttgart, 1988, pp. 328-340, 727-744.

Frondizi, R., "Are Truth and History Incompatible?" *Truth and Historicity,* H-G Gadamer (ed.), The Hague, 1972.

Funk, R. W., *Parables and Presence,* Philadelphia, 1982.

Gabbard, L. P., "The Pinter Surprise", *Harold Pinter,* Steven H. Gale (ed.), London and Ontario, 1976, pp. 175-187.

Gadamer, H-G., *Philosophical Hermeneutics,* Berkeley, Los Angeles and London, 1975.

————, *Truth and Method,* London 1965.

Gale, S. H., *Butter's Going Up: A Critical Analysis of Harold Pinter's Work,* London and Ontario, 1977.

Gehlen, A., *Anthropologische Forschung,* Hamburg, 1961.

George, K.E., *Rhythm in Drama,* Pittsburgh, 1975.

Geraint, J., *The Art and Truth of the Parables; A Study in Their Form and Modern Interpretation,* London, 1964.

Gordon, L., "Death of a Salesman: An Appreciation", *Twentieth Century Interpretations of Death of a Salesman,* H. W. Koon (ed.), New Jersey, 1983.

Habermas, J. H., *Strukturwandel der Öffentlichkeit,* Rein, 1968.

————, "Können komplexe Geselschaften eine Vernünftige Identität ausbilden", *Zwei Reden aus Anlass des Hegel-Preises,* J. H. Habermas and D. Heinrich (eds.), Frankfurt, 1974.

Habermas, J. and Luhman, N., *Theorie der Geselschaft oder Socialtechnologie,* Frankfurt, 1971.

Hadomi, L., "Fantasy and Reality: Dramatic Rhythm in 'Death of a Salesman'", *Modern Drama,* vol. xxxi, 2, 1988, pp. 157-174.

Hall, P., "Directing Pinter", *Harold Pinter: You Never Heard Such Silence,* A. Bold (ed.), London, 1985.

Harnisch, W., *Die gleichniserzählungen Jesu,* Göttingen, 1985.

Hayman, R., *Harold Pinter,* London, 1975.

Heitmann, H. D., "Dramaturgie des Raumes Eine Literarkritische Analyse an Hand von Harold Pinters Comedies of Menace", *Duisbürger Studies,* 8, Sankt Augustin, 1982.

Hinchcliffe, A. P., *Harold Pinter,* Twayne Publishing, USA, 1967.

Hollis, J. R., *Harold Pinter: The Poetics of Silence,* London, 1970.

Holtan, O., "Mythic Patterns in Ibsen's Last Plays", *Structural Anthropology*, C. Jacobson and B. Grundfest Schoepf, New York, 1967.

Hornby, R., *Patterns in Ibsen's Middle Plays*, New York, 1981.

Hudgins, C. C., "Intended Audience Response, 'The Homecoming' and the Ironic Mode of Identification", *Harold Pinter, Critical Approaches*, S. H. Gale (ed.), Dickinson University Press, 1985, pp. 102-118.

Huftel, S., *Arthur Miller: The Burning Glass*, New York, 1965.

Hugh, N., "'The Homecoming': Kith and Kin", *Modern British Dramatists*, Y. R. Brown (ed.), New York, 1968, pp. 145-163.

Hutter, M., *The Changing Family*, New York, 1981.

Jacobson, C., and Schoepf, B. G., *Structural Anthropology*, New York, 1967.

Jacobson, I., "Family Dreams in 'Death of a Salesman'", *American Literature* vol. 47, 1975-1976, pp. 247-257.

Jauss, H.R. *Toward an Aesthetic of Reception*, Brighton, 1982.

Jeremias, J., *Die Gleichnisse Jesus*, Göttingen, 1970.

Jiji, V. M., "Pinter's Four Dimensioned House: The Homecoming", *Modern Drama*, vol. 17, 1974.

Jung, C., *Psychology and Religion: West and East*, Princeton, 1969.

Kaiser, G. (ed.), *Die Dramen des Andreas Gryphius: Eine Sammlung von Einzelinterpretationen*, Stuttgart, 1968.

Kalkus, R. M., "Werthers Krankenheit zum Tode Pathalogie und Familie in der Empfindsamkeit", *Urscenen: Literaturwissenschaft als Diskursanalyse und Diskurskritik*, F. A. Kittler and H. Turk (eds.) Frankfurt, 1977.

Kennedy, A., *Dramatic Dialogue*, Cambridge, 1983.

————, "Ritualised Language", *Harold Pinter*, M. Scott (ed.), London, 1985, pp. 186-189.

Kissinger, Warren S., *The Parables of Jesus: A History of Interpretation and Bibliography*, New York and London, 1979.

Kittler, F. and Turk, H., *Urszenen Literaturwissenschaft als Diskursanalyse und Diskurstheorie*, Frankfurt, 1977.

Knowles, R., "Names and Naming in the Plays of Harold Pinter", *Harold Pinter: You Never Heard Such Silence*, A. Bold (ed.), London, 1984, pp. 113-131.

Kolakowski, L., *Die Gegenwärtigkeit des Mythos*, Munich, 1974.

Konrad, L. B., "Fathers' Sons and Mothers' Guilt: Dramatic responses to Darwin", *Themes in Drama*, Cambridge, 1985, pp. 137-149.

Koon, H. W., *Twentieth Century Interpretations of Death of a Salesman*, New Jersey, 1983.

Kreps, B., "Time and Harold Pinter's Possible Realities: Art as Life and Vice Versa", *Modern Drama*, vol. 22, 1979, pp. 47-60.

Krutch, J. W., *Modernism in Modern Drama*, New York, 1953.

Kushner, E., "Greek Myth in Modern Drama: Paths of Transformation", *Literary Criticism and Myth*, J. P. Strelka (ed.), University Park and London, 1980, pp. 198-209.

Lacan, J., *Ecrits*, Paris, 1966.

Lacan, J., *Ecrits*, New York and London, 1977.

———, *Schriften I*, Paris, 1966.

———, "Über eine Frage", *Schriften II*, Paris 1966.

Lang, H., *Die Sprache und das Unbewußte*, Frankfurt, 1973.

Langbaum, R., *The Mysteries of Identity*, New York, 1977.

Leland, C., "Ghosts seen from an Existential Aspect", *Ibsen Yearbook* vol. 13, 1973-1974, pp. 118-126.

———, "In Defense of Pastor Manders", *Modern Drama*, vol. 21, 1978, pp. 405-420.

Levin, R., *The Multiple Plot in English Renaissance Drama*, Chicago and London, 1971.

Levi-Strauss, C., "The Structural Study of Myth", *Myth: A Symposium*, T. A. Sebeok (ed.), Bloomington, Indiana, 1958, pp. 81-106.

Levitt, P. M., *A Structural Approach to the Analysis of Drama*, The Hague and Paris, 1971.

Lucas, L., *Dialogstrukturen*, Bonn, 1968.

Luhman, N., *Legitimation durch Verfahren*, Neuweid un Berlin, 1969.

———, *Vertrauen*, Stuttgart, 1973.

Lyons, C. R., "Character and Theatrical Space", in James Redmond (ed.), *Theme in Drama*, Cambridge, 1987, pp. 26-44.

———, *Henrik Ibsen. The Divided Consciousness*, London and Amsterdam, 1972.

Man (de), P., *Allegories of Reading*, New Haven and London, 1979.

Manheim, M., *Eugene O'Neill: New Language of Kinship,* Syracuse University Press, 1982.

Marranca, B. (ed.), *American Dreams - The Imagination of Sam Shepard,* New York, 1981

McCarthy, G., *Edward Albee,* Hampshire and London, 1987.

McMahon, H. M., "Arthur Miller's Common Man: The Problem of the Realistic and the Mythic", unpublished PhD dissertation, Purdue University, 1972.

Mengel, E., *Harold Pinters Dramen im Spiegel der Sociologischen Rollentheorie,* Frankfurt, Bern, Las Vegas, 1978.

Meyer, H. G., *Henrik Ibsen,* New York, 1972.

Middleton, D. and Edwards, D. (eds.), *Collective Remembering,* London, 1990.

Miller, A., *Arthur Miller's Collected Plays,* Introduction,vol. 1, New York, 1965.

Morris, K., "The Homecoming", *Tulane Drama Review* vol 11,2, Winter 1966.

Mottram, R., *Inner Landscapes - The Theatre of Sam Shepard,* Columbia, 1984.

Murphy, B., *American Realism and American Drama 1880-1940,* Cambridge, 1987.

Nash, T., "Sam Shepard's Buried Child: The Ironic Use of Folklore", *Modern Drama,* vol. xxvi, 4, 1983, pp. 415-423.

Nash, W, A., *The Homecoming Motif in Selected Works of Eugene O'Neill,* University of Utah, 1975.

Nelson, B., *Der Ursprung der Moderne,* Frankfurt, 1984.

Nelson, R. J., *Play Within A Play,* New Haven, 1958.

Northam, J., *Ibsen: A Critical Study,* Cambridge, 1973.

Orbison, T., "Mythic Levels in Shepard's 'True West'", *Modern Drama,* vol. xxvii, 1984, pp. 506-519.

Orr, J., *Tragic Drama and Modern Society,* London, 1981.

Paolucci, A., *From Tension to Tonic, The Plays of Edward Albee,* London and Amsterdam, 1972.

Parker, B., "Point of View in Arthur Miller's 'Death of a Salesman'", *Twentieth Century Interpretations of "Death of a Salesman",* H. W. Koon (ed.), New Jersey, 1983, pp. 41-55.

Pavel, T. G., "The Poetics of Plot", *The Case of English Renaissance Drama*, Manchester University, 1985.

Pavis, P., "The Classical Heritage of Modern Drama; The Case of Post Modern Theatre", *Modern Drama*, vol. xxix, 1, 1986, pp. 1-22.

Pfister, M., *The Theory and Analysis of Drama*, Cambridge, 1988.

Pinter, H., "Writing for the Theatre", *Evergreen Review*, vol. 8, 1968.

Platz, N. H., "The Social Significance of Locality in British Drama from the 1950s to the 1970s", in *Modern Drama and Society*, Hans-Jürgen Diller (Hrsg.), Heidelberg, 1983, pp. 67-83.

Porter, T. E., *Myth and Modern American Drama*, Detroit, 1969.

Postelwait, T. E., *The Design of the Past: Uses of Memory in the Drama of Henrik Ibsen, Samuel Beckett and Harold Pinter*, University of Minnesota, 1976.

Postelwait, T. E. (ed.), *William Archer on Ibsen: The Major Essays 1889-1919*, Connecticut and London, 1984.

Putzel, S., "Expectation, Confutation, Revelation: Audience Complicity in the plays of Sam Shepard", *Modern Drama*, vol. xxx, 2, 1987, pp. 147-160.

Quigley, A. E., *The Pinter Problem*, Princeton, 1975.

Rabillard, S., "Sam Shepard: Theatrical Power and American Dream", *Modern Drama* vol. xxx no. 1, March 1984, pp.58-71.

Rengstorf, K. H., *Die Re-Investiture des verlorenen Sohnes in der Gleichniserzählung Jesus, Luk 15, 11-32*, Köln und Oplanden, 1967.

Rosen, C., *Plays of Impasse*, Princeton, 1983.

Ross, J. F., *Portraying Analogy*, Cambridge, 1981.

Roudane, M. C., *Understanding Edward Albee*, University of South Carolina, 1987.

Roy, E., "'Who's Afraid of Virginia Woolf?' and the Tradition", *Critical Essays on Edward Albee*, P. C. Kolin and J. Madison Davis (eds.), Boston, 1986.

Rutenberg, M. E., *Edward Albee: Playwright in Protest*, New York, 1969.

Scanlan, T., *Family, Drama and American Dreams*, Connecticut, 1978.

Schäfer, K.K. *Handlung im neueren Britischen Drama*, Frankfurt/M, 1985.

Schelsky, H., *Die Skeptische Generation*, Düsseldorf and Cologne, 1957.

Schlueter, J., *Metafictional Characters in Modern Drama*, New York, 1979.

Schniewind, J., *Das Gleichnis vom verlorenen Sohn, Göttingen*, 1940.

Schöne, A., *Säkularisation als sprachbildende Kraft*, Göttingen, 1968.

Schweckendieck, A., *Bühnengeschichte des Verlorenen Sohnes in Deutschland*, vol. I, Leipzig, 1930.

Scringeour, J. R., "From Loving to the Misbegotten: Despair in the Drama of Eugene O'Neill", *Modern Drama* vol. 20, 1977 pp. 37-54.

Shorter, E., *The Making of the Modern Family*, New York, 1975.

————, *Die Geburt der modernen Family*, Reinbeck, 1977.

Skloot, R., "Warpath and Boulevards: Sam Shepard on the Road of American Non-Realism", *Assaph*, Section C 3, Tel Aviv, 1986, pp. 207-213.

Stannard, D. E., "Changes in the American Family: Fiction and Reality", in *Changing Images of the Family*, V. Tufte and B. Myerhoff (eds.), New Haven and London, 1979, pp. 83-98.

States, R. O., "Homecoming: The Shock of Non-Recognition", *Hudson Review* vol. 21, 1968-1969, pp. 474-486.

Stockum (von), T. C., *Das Jedermann-Motiv und das Motiv des Verlorenen Sohnes in Niederlandischen und Niederdeutschen Drama*, Amsterdam, 1958.

Strassner, M., *Analytisches Drama*, Munich, 1980.

Strelka, J. P. (ed.), *Literary Criticism and Myth*, University Park and London, 1980.

Sundquist, E. J., *Home as Found Authority and Genealogy in Nineteenth Century American Literature*, Baltimore and London, 1979.

Sykes, A., *Harold Pinter*, Queensland, 1972.

Szondi, P., *Theory of the Modern Drama*, Cambridge, 1987.

Thompson, D. T., *Pinter, the Player's Playwright*, London, 1985.

Tiusanen, T., *O'Neill's Scenic Images*, Princeton, 1968.

Tobin, P. D., *Time and the Novel*, Princeton, 1978.

Tolbert, M. A., "The Prodigal Son: An Essay in Literary Criticism from a Psychoanalytical Perspective", *Polyvalent Narration*, J. D. Crossan (ed.), *Semeia* 9, University of Montana, 1977, pp. 1-21.

Tornquist, E., *A Drama of Souls*, Uppsala, 1968.

————, "Jesus and Judas: On Biblical Allusions in O'Neill's Plays", *Etudes Anglaises* vol. 24, 1, 1971, pp. 41-49.

Trench, Archbishop, *Notes On The Parables of Our Lord*, London, n.d.

Via, D. D. (Jr.), "The Prodigal Son: A Jungian Reading", *Polyvalent Narration,* J. D. Crossan (ed.), *Semeia* 9, University of Montana, 1977.

Voelker, P. D. "Eugene O'Neill's Aesthetics of Drama", *Modern Drama,* vol. xx 1978, pp. 87-109.

——————, "O' Neill's First Families" in "Games People Play: Family Relationships in O'Neill", *The Eugene O'Neill Newsletter,* Summer-Fall 1987, pp. 13-19.

Wardle, I., "The Territorial Struggle", *Harold Pinter: A Casebook,* M. Scott (ed.), London, 1986.

Watts, H., "Myth and Drama", *Perspectives on Drama,* J. L. Calderwood and H. E. Toliver (eds.),New York, 1968, pp. 112-135.

Westermann, S. *Die Krise der Familie bei Edward Albee,* Heidelberg, 1974.

White, J. J., "Mythological Fiction and the Reading Process", *Literary Criticism and Myth,* J. P. Strelka (ed.), University Park and London, 1980, pp. 72-92.

Whiting, C. G., "Digging Up Buried Child", *Modern Drama* vol. xxxi, 4, 1988, pp. 548-556.

Williams, G. J., "The Dreamy Kid: O'Neill's Darker Brother", *Theater Annual,* vol. 43, 1988, pp. 3-14.

Wilson, A., "Fool of Desire: The Spectator to the Plays of Sam Shepard", *Modern Drama,* vol. xxx, 1, March 1987, pp.46-57.

Young, A. R., *The English Prodigal Son Plays to 1625,* Salzburg, 1979.

INDEX

INDEX